LET YOUR BUSINESS
BURN

LET YOUR BUSINESS
BURN

STOP PUTTING OUT FIRES, DISCOVER PURPOSE, AND BUILD A BUSINESS THAT MATTERS

SCOTT BEEBE

DEDICATION

To Ashley:
Your optimistic truth delivers life
to my fragmented mind.

CONTENTS

Foreword
by Dan Miller

Ah, yes—the appeal of having my own business. No boss looking over my shoulder, no clock to punch, no meaningless meetings. I get to build my own dream, and there's no ceiling on income. What could possibly be wrong with this picture?

I hate to admit it, but I drifted into my business. It grew out of a Sunday school class as those attending asked for more resources and time. Gradually, I had a full-time business. But because it grew from my volunteer ministry, I didn't approach it like a normal business. I didn't identify my vision or my mission or my core values. I just started providing what my customers wanted. My income was more than my expenses, so I assumed I had a real business.

Making money was not my primary goal. Rather, money showed up because I wanted to continue to serve people well by guiding their talents into work that was meaningful, fulfilling, and profitable.

I was fortunate in how things were working pretty well.

New products were being added, client testimonials were flowing in, and revenues were growing nicely. But somewhere along the line, I felt like I lost control of my business. Although I loved what I was doing, I was working far too many hours. My health began to suffer. Instead of jumping out of bed eager to get to work, I found that I was fatigued and worn out by 10:00 AM.

And then I met Scott Beebe.

He gently walked me through identifying a clear vision. Then we moved on to mission and core values. We clarified the key roles in the company, including my own. I learned how to delegate rather than doing it myself because it was easier than taking the time to show someone else. We built a timeline for prioritized accomplishments. I witnessed that "freedom from" opens the door to "freedom to."

Yes, I resisted all the "structure" and new work but agreed to try and see. It seemed this was akin to the cobbler's son having no shoes. I could coach others on doing these things but was just too busy to do them in my own business. Yes, it stretched me. But like the struggle of the butterfly getting out of the cocoon, these struggles are part of the process of making our businesses run smoothly. And like the butterfly's situation, those struggles are not intended to limit or cripple us or to keep us in the building stage forever but to allow us to develop our strongest skills, resilience, fortitude, personal excellence, and wealth over time.

Suddenly, things began to change. I found I already had the people in place to delegate more effectively. I experimented with being in charge but not in control. I increased my number of free days where I totally unplugged from my work. At the end of the next full year, I realized that I had taken more time off than ever before, and felt like I had slowed down considerably, but net profit was up by almost 300 percent.

In Let Your Business Burn, Scott proposes real solutions and business strategies that are available to all of us. I commend you on taking advantage of this intimate look inside the thinking, systems, and practices of highly successful business owners. By modeling the behavior of those you are about to see in these pages and understanding your own "Road Map," you too can put yourself firmly on the path from which there's no turning back, and you will "Stop Putting Out Fires, Discover Purpose, and Build a Business That Matters."

FOREWORD
BY AARON WALKER

Historically, I do not schedule one-on-one meetings with potential clients until I have thoroughly checked them out. You get a lot of guys just wanting to "pick your brain." However, midday on a Friday, early one April, I found myself sitting at a small round table in the center of a Starbucks on West End Ave in Nashville, Tennessee, waiting on a guy named Scott Beebe. My first thought was *How will I know it's him?* My next thought was *What is my exit strategy?*

Well, it was pretty easy to identify him. Backpack slung over one shoulder, walking with a definite purpose, and this huge smile that said, "Somebody please shake my hand." Wow, was I pleasantly surprised. My exit-strategy mindset quickly diminished, and a new long-term relationship was birthed.

Scott hired me as his personal and professional coach to add an additional layer of success and significance to his arsenal of amazing attributes. We worked diligently every week to fine-tune a dream that lay just beneath the surface. I recognized quickly something unusual was developing. I could not articulate in words to others what I saw, but I could sense a passion deep inside of Scott that was longing to be released. We all have heard that it's impossible to read the label when we are in the jar. That's exactly where Scott was: he just needed me to read the label.

Fast-forward five years. The student is now the teacher. That's right, the roles are reversed. Scott is now our team leader. The mission, vision, and values are all attributed to the narrow brilliance of a guy who sixty months earlier was mooching a free grande caramel macchiato. I'm a veteran entrepreneur of forty years. I've owned a dozen businesses and had hundreds of people work for me, but never have I encountered an individual with such a deep passion for eliminating chaos from their life equipped with a systematic approach to accomplish such a feat.

Processes and systems were foreign to me. This was something I thought everyone else needed, not I. I pushed back relentlessly at every turn. After all, I've made it this far. I had made it this far using sheer grit and determination, not fully realizing there was a better way. Talk about putting out fires—it was my #1 daily task. Finally, after much debate, Scott encouraged me to systematize my business. I went to the local Walgreens, bought a bottle of Tylenol, and let him know I was ready to start. (I still have the unopened bottle.)

Scott walked me through a step-by-step process, painful at times, but a very methodical approach that has revolutionized my life. I kept telling him that while we were toying with all this minutia, my business was burning down. He said, "Let it burn!"

What? Let it burn?

He promised that if I would take the time to delegate, automate, or possibly even eliminate some things, I would end up with a sustainable business that would pay dividends for generations. I'm here today as a living testament that following Scott's system radically improved the way we approach everything. Now I have the margin to work *on* my business instead of *in* my business, and we are experiencing 35 to 40 percent annual growth. I'm glad I let my business burn.

—Aaron Walker

founder of View from the Top

INTRODUCTION

CHAOS HATES YOU AND IS ALREADY WAITING TO DESTROY YOU.

Chaos thrives in stress, anxiety, fractured relationships, frustrated spouses, and emotionally removed kids. The majority of small-business owners are being overrun by hundreds of little chaos fires; payroll, hiring, taxes, lines of credit, customers, products, and marketing.

The good news is that you are not alone, and there is a way for you to conquer the chaos fires in your small business.

The sage Greek professor Dr. Curtis Vaughan pointed his crooked hand into the face of our collective class one morning and declared, "If you are down to your last dollar, and you have the option to buy food or buy books . . . buy books."

Thomas Friedman, the respected *New York Times* columnist and long-time Middle Eastern correspondent has recently hypothesized that "because of the explosive power of exponential growth, the twenty-first century will be equivalent to 20,000 years of progress at today's rate of progress."

That rate of progress is a societal sprint. It only and ironically heightens the value of this book. It also heightens the chaos. Books are wise teachers that never retire. They escort us on adventures that our minds alone would never dare to take.

Why this book?

Barnes and Noble has served on two occasions as a foundational ground zero for major mind-expanding moments in my life. The first took place after returning from Vietnam on a two-week preceptorship with my mentor Bob Roberts. We met for lunch to debrief. After eating, we ran over to Barnes and Noble in the mid-cities of North Texas, and he picked out six or seven books on multiple topics in multiple genres.

Two of the books that Bob bought for me that day have taken up residence in my top five all-time books: Dallas Willard's **The Divine Conspiracy** and Thomas L. Friedman's *The World Is Flat*. Books on both religion and globalization existed prior to Willard and Friedman authoring their books, but religion and globalization *from their perspective* did not yet exist. These two books were a virtual passport granting my mind and soul access to territory that had been foreign to me.

The second transformative moment came at a Barnes and Noble in Knoxville, Tennessee, when someone suggested that I read Michael Gerber's *E-Myth Revisited*. That book clicked with me and awakened my language of systems and processes. The E-Myth idea resonated with me as I had a knack for helping people make important transitions in their businesses.

Both of those pivotal moments came through books. This book has the potential to become your friend and counselor and serve as a teacher for your business. To my knowledge, there does not exist another book stewing the three ingredients of global in-the-trench stories, overly pragmatic step-by-step procedures, and a massive focus on as-you-go implementation written by a small-business owner who battles chaos each day. This book merges all three to provide a tasty and nutritious mind meal that you will be able to chew on for the entirety of your work life. It can serve as a reference and a principled anchor in the world of strategic tides.

Even though I have mastered some things and teach them to others, I am still a down-to-earth kind of guy. I prefer mid-priced generic travel pants, enjoy hamburgers cooked rare, drive used cars, and hear the voice of fear almost daily.

I also operate from a mind of whimsy fueled by implementation. My company focuses on making great things happen as we liberate small-business owners from their chaos.

We developed a mascot named Implementation, which is a bicycle-riding unicorn on a rainbow-colored towel.

Why? Because unicorns *do* exist, and they look just like work. So, let's dive in and ride the unicorn.

Liberation From Chaos

Chaos wants you to believe there is no way out, but that is not true. Chaos shows up in hundreds of little fires that all look urgent, and yet most of them are not. This book will walk you step by step down the path to liberation from feeling the need to extinguish every chaos fire that is set. Implement a new strategy, and the fires of chaos may continue on, leaving you perplexed. Implement an established principle, and you will begin to ignore the fires of chaos, declaring, "I know you are here, and I will not relent in pursuing our purpose!"

An irritated and frustrated client called one day and decided that I made for a good punching bag. He said, "You say that we can be liberated from chaos, but I don't think you can liberate me from chaos because chaos is all around and will always be around."

It was a crisis moment for me over the next seven days, because the very mission that we have devoted ourselves to is liberating small-business owners from the chaos of working in their business. Working *in* your business is having your head down in emails, picking the weeds of data entry, invoicing, and other tasks that other people could do, but you will not let them.

I called the client back and with a fervor that is rare for me to muster. I simply said, "You are wrong."

"About what?"

I launched in. "The other day, you told me that you could not be liberated from chaos because chaos will always be around. You are right in saying that chaos will always be around, but you are absolutely not right in saying that you cannot be liberated from chaos."

His response was, "Huh. That makes sense."

Addiction is one source of chaos. A friend and client, Will Dalzell, has built a beautiful family and a successful landscape design and construction business. At one time, he was being controlled by powerful drugs, and he spent time in prison. While he could still have access to that lifestyle, he has chosen to be liberated from the drugs that once had control over him.

Hard drugs and other harmful things are always around. They are always available, but we never have to submit ourselves to them. Other friends of mine have been subjected to the damaging control of excessive alcohol, and they have been liberated.

Charles William Eliot, Harvard's longest tenured President and the man who transformed the college into a research juggernaut said, "Books are the quietest and most constant of friends; they are the most accessible and wisest of counselors and the most patient of teachers." Wise thoughts from a man who endured the chaos of his father's lost fortune.

Thomas Jefferson, enduring the chaos and unknown of the American Revolution, famously declared, "I cannot live without books." Neither can we. Books have provided access, counsel, and opportunity to Jefferson, Eliot, and thousands of entrepreneurs who take the time to explore their pages. May this book be the friend you need in your business and give you the courage to let those chaos fires burn while you pursue building a business on purpose. First, let's look at what I consider to be the biggest lie in business and find out what the truth really is.

THE BIGGEST LIE IN BUSINESS: "IT'S JUST BUSINESS"

"It's just business" is a scapegoat for not having to express emotion when we need to make a hard decision related to work. If you snub a client or employee on a project, the short-term fix is to simply hang it on the rack of "It's just business." We have all heard people say it. We may even have said it ourselves. But it is not true.

When you hire or fire someone, their emotions and responses follow them home. When something exciting or terrible is going on at home, their emotions and responses follow them to work.

My mind is constantly employing itself with home, family, work, faith, political, and global thoughts, and a variety of others at 3:37 A.M. on a Tuesday when I am trying to sleep and at 2:21 P.M. on a Wednesday when I am trying to work.

Business and life intersect, and they are continually connected. One of the purposes of business is to serve us in life, and one of the purposes of life is to work and use our skill sets as a means to serve others.

Business is not an isolated silo where we escape from the reality of everything else going on in our life. Business *is* a part of that life, and it is a powerful way to live out the "narrow brilliance" that God uniquely designed you with. Business sits at the intersection of our family, faith, relationships, politics, and a variety of regular life events that happen every day.

You have heard people say, "I keep work at work." That is impossible and naïve. The mind is both a play-by-play sports announcer and a bad roommate who will not be quiet. As we progress through daily life, our mind narrates the world.

That is a cool tree.

You did not finish your email before you left.

Your bank account is running dangerously low.

Your daughter wishes you would spend more time with her.

Mmm, that steak is delicious!

Those thoughts do not magically suspend when we go to work as if our mind acts in a silo.

The sharpest minds in the world create and leverage maps to navigate complex explorations. Through thousands of face-to-face, in-the-trench coaching hours, I have developed a principle-based road map that holds amidst the shifting tides of strategy. That road map is the Four Steps to Business Freedom.

As you begin your adventure into the Four Steps to Business Freedom, know that every element of your life somehow touches business and vice versa.

It is not just business. Business affects everything. Having and maintaining the right perspective is paramount.

My Promise to You

We as humans facilitate the doubling of computing technology every two years or so (Moore's Law), and our minds speed up to maintain composure. Books necessarily slow us down and allow us to identify and conquer chaos.

Slowing down to the biased twenty-first-century human seems to be an inefficient stewardship of time, and yet it is the kind of quiet that Jesus would retire to in order to hear the voice of God.

I promise as you read this book, you will slow down. I promise as you implement the principles in this book, you will see transformation. I promise as you create habits from the coaching of this book, you will begin to experience liberation from the chaos of working in your small business and be equipped to help others implement the same.

The privilege and responsibility of small-business ownership did not enter my life until I was thirty-nine years old. I am a late bloomer to this steep and largely unpredictable roller coaster. The accounting does not entirely make sense to me either. The marketing continues to be elusive squirrels sprinting in unparalleled directions. The voices scream in my head also.

I am very much like you except for one advantage that you will never have. That might sound like an arrogant statement, but it is not. It is just a simple, true statement, and here is why: I have perspective on *you* that you cannot have because you are you, and I am not. That is one of the ways you benefit by having a business coach. A coach sees what you cannot.

The first section of this book is a priority because it allows me to speak directly to you from the perspective of a business coach.

Business coaching is not the same as traditional business consulting. Consultants have years of experience in your specific industry. Coaches likely do not. Consultants have reams of notes on best practices from similar businesses. Coaches likely do not. Consultants usually offer sage advice regardless of the implementation of that advice. A business coach's passions need not be tied to a specific industry but are tied instead to passionately studying the game of business.

A business coach works *with you* in the trenches to develop a game plan and then stands within earshot to make sure you implement what was designed. Some business owners even have me lead their regular team meetings! A business coach makes sure that you show up for practice every day and pushes you to limits well beyond what you thought possible. A business coach encourages you when you get your mind pummeled, confronts you when you extend an invitation to your own pity party, and rejoices with childlike zeal when you execute and score!

You might be thinking, "Okay, great. But I don't really think I need a coach."

In a brilliant 2013 *TED talk*, Bill Gates famously begins by declaring, "Everyone needs a coach."

Eric Schmidt said the best advice he ever received was from a Google board member who simply said, "You need a coach."

You need a coach, and this book will help facilitate meeting that need. If you need help beyond this book, l please feel free to reach out at *burn@mybusinessonpurpose.com.*

I promise that if you implement what you are about to experience, you and your small business—dare I say even your family—will experience a freedom that is unattainable without the discipline of implementation. The stories that I will share with you will illustrate the important principles in this book.

TJ's Story

TJ has implemented what you are about to read. He was able to be home *and* be present with greater regularity while profitability increased through accountable processes. That growth led to increased profits, and now his wife Rachel is living out her dream of being a stay-at-home mom for their two boys.

TJ has a hard-driving ("D" on the DISC profile) personality with a bull-in-a-china-shop mentality. TJ has never met a concrete wall that he could not run straight through. A "D" personality is quick to act and slow to take in all of the data that other personalities would before making decisions. TJ has been in the spray foam industry since 2004, and founded Atlantic Spray Foam in 2012, under the mantra that you could "Call TJ."

With great sincerity, he wanted to be the spray foam contractor that customers could call directly. Of course, that mindset created a natural bottleneck that was not only forcing the business to run less efficiently, but it was also forcing TJ to spend less time at home with Rachel and the boys.

Like many approaches that need to be course corrected, the implementation of what is needed to work *on* your business is not easy. It takes focused work, much like writing this book. It is Wednesday as I am writing this section. Wednesdays are loaded with one-on-one client meetings, and this is one of the most exciting days of my week—a day spent with small-business heroes. A few weeks ago, our Business On Purpose (BOP) virtual team really challenged me about an action item that we had on our weekly Action Items sheet—a simple spreadsheet that acts as a digital whiteboard where we track progress on tasks. Go to MyBusinessOnPurpose.com/tools if you would like to implement one for you and your team). The item?

"Write the book and get it to a publisher."

I was going to scrap the item and move on to other things, but Jessie, a meek and kind team member, piped up in rare form and simply said, "I disagree." Huh? Jessie? Disagreeing? She then went on to say, "I think you need to set aside time to write, and isn't that why you set the new three-week coaching schedule?"

That was accountability like a straight punch to the nose.

She was right. That was why we adjusted our coaching schedule. We blocked off today, Wednesday, for me to sit in a hammock on the edge of a tidal creek marsh here in the Lowcountry of South Carolina and continue to write. No phone. No email. No distractions.

It has been hard.

While our family was away for spring break to the canyons of the Southwest, my boys and I decided to hike to Angels Landing in the Zion National Park. It is a long climb to a place that many would look upon curiously and remark on my irresponsibility as a parent. Close to the end of the hike, our only option was a one-lane "trail" that people hike holding on to a chain with no backup plan. On this trail, all of us are just one hard slip away from careening down the side of a cliff where devastation awaits.

More than ninety-five percent of the hike was either straining uphill or managing the impact going downhill with very few flat and smooth sections. It was hard. Not Navy SEAL hard or delivering a baby hard, but hard in a way that taxes a person physically, emotionally, and other ways.

Writing this book requires time with uphill and downhill segments, and you will experience the same by reading this book.

I used to think a person worked hard, hit a certain "jackpot" moment, and then coasted to the end. Now I realize that effort and implementation will always be a part of life. Your investment of time and effort will be rewarded.

Are you ready to do the hard things and take one step at a time to be liberated from the chaos of working *in* your business doing the day-to-day tasks so you can work *on* your business? Working *on* your business is maneuvering through high-level, principle-based decisions (think vision, mission, and values) and delegation. Follow me, implement, and we will take you there.

I hope you are stretched and ready to meet my Nigerian Muslim friend who speaks five languages.

You Need A Common Language

My friend Muhammed speaks five languages: English, French, Fulfulde, Hausa, and Yoruba. I speak one: English (although I know enough Yoruba and Hausa to make local Nigerians grin). It is our common language.

Due to some of the nuances of Muhammed's life and travels, he has embraced various cultures and the languages that go with them. Muhammed has a background that I do not fully understand, and yet it has provided him opportunities out of my grasp. He is one of his father's thirty-seven children. His dad has four wives and is the emir of a geographic territory in Nigeria. Although we have massive differences, Muhammed and I are able to communicate because we have a common language.

As American English speakers, we may find it easy to allow our societal and economic superpower status to serve as an excuse to lock in on our one language and save the energy from learning anything new. Today, English is the "common language" throughout the world (although not the most-spoken native language).

If there is one superpower that I wish could be bestowed on me, it would be the ability to fluently speak the language of anyone I encounter. I would like to go beyond *Welcome*, *Willkommen*, *Bienvenue*, *Buenos Dias*, and *E'Karo*. *Hello* and *goodbye* are a good start, though. They lay the groundwork for what comes next.

When I do not speak your language, it is more challenging to speak to you the way you wish to be spoken to. Speaking to others the way they wish to be spoken to is the bedrock of building a business that propels toward the vision.

Throughout history, there have been bedrock languages that serve as "common languages across cultures.""Greek was officially known as the "lingua franca" of the Roman Empire, and thus scholars and merchants chose to speak their native language while also having at least functional Greek in their back pocket.

A common language shortens the time of decision-making, innovation, understanding, and collaboration. In your business, if you wish to connect and communicate well with each other as a team and progress toward your vision, it is imperative that you have a common language. Cultures have a common language. Sports teams have a common language, part of which is found in a playbook. Computer programmers around the world have common language in their respective codes. Common languages are the connected interstates of society, business, family, marriage, and parenting.

Consider this book your business language tutor that facilitates a common language in your business.

Installing and implementing words like *vision, mission, values, systems, processes, team meetings, weekly schedules,* and *12-week plans* will position you and your team with a predictable playbook that will allow you to call the plays in real time and set expectations for everyone.

A Story of Perspective

The Maple Leaf was his home flag, and yet his childhood was marked by heat, outdoor kitchens, pounded yam, and the adventure of life in the West African country of Nigeria. Don Campion grew up as a child of a missionary couple and was raised with one eye on culture and the other on adventure.

Calvin Buliske (Cal) was Don's local missionary mentor. Cal was a classic West African missionary who had all of the looks of the Marlboro man and the tenderness of a thoughtful mentor. Cal served as a missionary through the SIM (at the time called Sudan Interior Mission) sending agency, and he was an adventurer. He was a skilled tradesman who worked to build Titcombe College in Egbe, Kogi State, a well-respected educational institution in Nigeria at the time. Titcombe has since fed Nigeria with a powerful stream of private and public leaders who have gone on to serve the nation.

Cal's lure was the dynamism and wild-hair ideas that he developed as he carved out a bush swimming pool in the side of a mountain or modified motorcycles and go-karts for the kids to enjoy. Don embraced Cal's dynamism. When it was time for Don to head off to university back in North America, boarding a ship from Nigeria was the most cost-effective return transportation available to Don.

He chose instead to create an adventure that quite literally would be paralleled by very few Western men during his time. Don harnessed his own emerging trade skills and modified a Honda 150 motorcycle outfitting the machine with 20 gallons worth of fuel tanks and creating holding satchels for his gear.

Don prepared his route, packed his gear, fueled up, fired up the modified Honda, and took off on a daring discovery crossing the Sahara desert from Nigeria in the South to Morocco in the North, across the Straits of Gibraltar up through Spain and France, and then finally across the English channel into England, where he would ditch the Honda and then board a ship to Canada.

When Don shared this story with me, he revealed pictures of his journey and explained his simple method of navigation. There is a series of markers throughout the Sahara that are placed as a route guide directing desert nomads through the trade routes of the barren tapestry. As Don progressed from marker to marker, he wrestled with the heat during the day and argued with the cold at night.

The great desert is an unrelenting fighter that will take you through twelve hard rounds and continue to land consistent sucker punches without mercy. As Don dealt his left hooks to the insistence of the desert, the Sahara was always prepared to fight back with a creative counterpunch all too familiar to so many who have decided to challenge the African champion.

The sun's thermal blanket was wide open one day, and Don was exhausted and thirsty. Looking ahead across the flat geography, Don was relieved to see a real-life oasis in the desert. He could finally get some rest, fill up his mind, and relieve his fatigue.

The closer he got, the more excited he became until finally he reached the destination to find nothing. The waves of water that he saw in his mind were waves of relenting heat laughing at Don's weakness.

What Don saw had little to do with reality. The elements, the angle, and the mind were all in sync to provide Don a picture of something that was not there. It was just a mirage.

In our business, our life, our home, politics, and in dealing with our neighbors, we think we see things in full perspective.

Perspective is "the art of drawing solid objects on a two-dimensional surface so as to give the right impression of their height, width, depth, and position in relation to each other when viewed from a particular point."

Don did not have full perspective in front of him. Don was limited by his location.

What would have helped Don was the perspective of a map, a friend up ahead, signage, or something outside of Don that had another angle on what he could see.

Today Don is a nomad of a different sort. He founded and owns Banyan Air, a fixed-base operation, located at the Ft. Lauderdale Executive Airport. He serves a mobile clientele with excellence and perspective. Don, his wife Sueanne, and his sister Betsie are still very much involved in Egbe, Kogi State, Nigeria today as the leaders of the Egbe Hospital Revitalization project (*egbehospital.org*).

"Without counsel, plans fail, but with many advisers they succeed" (Proverbs 15:22), because advisors offer perspective.

Business owners are notorious for pulling themselves up by their bootstraps.

"Just doing it myself."

"Going at it alone."

"Making my own way."

You do not have to. In fact, there is short-lived nobility in the Lone Ranger mindset. For what is life without others to share it with? The irony of Lone Ranger is that he is defiant of the "lone" title. Even he had a sidekick.

The perspective of others is a powerful resource in the toolbox of a business owner.

For the last few years, I have been a member in Aaron Walker's Iron Sharpens Iron mastermind group.

As I had listened to a variety of podcasts as a means to grow and develop personally, professionally, and spiritually, I was introduced to Aaron Walker and the idea of a mastermind group. A mastermind is a choice selection of people, usually fewer than ten, who meet in person or virtually to brainstorm and to support each other in their pursuits. Many successful people throughout history have been involved in groups like this.

Aaron, along with Dan Miller, Ken Abraham, Dave Ramsey, and others have been in a mastermind group in Nashville for about 20 years. They all rave about the value and benefits that their time together provided largely in part due to the perspective that each brought the others.

Other leaders of note were members of similar groups. Ben Franklin had the Junto group, Henry Ford and Thomas Edison had the Vagabonds, and J.R.R. Tolkien and C.S. Lewis had the Inklings.

There is challenge and accountability that comes along with the development of such a group, and yet perspective is nearly impossible without outsiders peering into the item of your focus at the time.

You see a lamp in front of you. The angle at which you are standing in relation to the lamp affords you the greatest opportunity to see the lamp from that angle. The problem is that there are a variety of other angles by which the lamp *can* be seen and *should* be seen in order for you to fully understand the attributes of the lamp.

Say, for instance, that you saw the lamp and thought, "This is the perfect accent to the interior of this room."

Your friend walks into the other side of the room, sees a different angle of the lamp, and realizes that someone has attached a bomb to that side of the lamp in an attempt to destroy your home.

Your view of the lamp changes because you are able to see a different perspective from your friend's angle.

We face millions of decisions every day. We will respond to many of those decisions with a singular perspective. For many decisions, that is okay such as brushing your teeth prior to taking a shower or vice versa. Perspective in that decision is not as crucial as the decision of paying increased taxes *or* purchasing capital equipment at the end of your fiscal year. Remember, "Without counsel, plans fail, but with many advisers they succeed" (Proverbs 15:22).

When you have the proper perspective, others now help remind you that it is never "just business."

"It's just business" is our attempt to create a scapegoat so that we do not have to feel emotion when we need to make a hard decision related to work. If you snub a client or employee on a project, the short-term fix is to hang it on the rack of "It's just business." Remember that business and life intersect. They are continually connected. A purpose of business is to serve us in life, and one of the purposes of life is to work and use our skill sets as a means to serve others whereby both can profit.

As you begin your adventure into Four Steps to Business Freedom, know that every element of your life somehow touches business and vice versa. Business is not an isolated silo where we escape from the reality of everything else going on in our life. Business *is* a part of that life and it *is* a powerful way to live out the "narrow brilliance" that God uniquely designed you with.

On a business trip to New Orleans, my wife Ashley and I traveled together. She spent the day at The Quarter Stitch, a quaint needlepoint and knitting shop where the ladies welcome in anyone who is interested in learning how to knit. After just a few hours, Ashley had merged into a hobby that she was fascinated by and semi-obsessed with for a season of life. For a few months after that business trip, we had a stash of knit hats as wearables for our family and gifts for our friends. Ashley would sit for hours and move those knitting needles back and forth, up and around, to craft scarfs and hats of all kinds. Knitting is rhythmic and methodical, thoughtful and deliberate, creative and artistic. It is said that God "formed (your) inward parts and knitted (you) together in your mother's womb" (Psalm 139:13). You are knitted into a certain pattern and wired in a certain way.

It is time for you to take that creative wiring you have been given and leverage it through the stage of business so that others will receive the joy of your product.

It is not *just business*. Your business process and practice should be and can be in direct connection with your personal knitting . . . the way you have been created. It is all connected, and I want to help you gain that necessary *perspective*.

LET YOUR BUSINESS BURN

As I have coached hundreds of heroic small-business owners over thousands of hours in conference rooms, restaurant tables, phone calls, and virtual meetings around the world, a pattern has emerged. The pattern is one of principle and less of strategy. Principles endure whereas strategies come and go. We like to say that principles eat strategies for breakfast. I have documented my journey of coaching and catalogued these principles into a powerful working dashboard we call Four Steps to Business Freedom. The modules that make up the Four Steps to Business Freedom are what we have found to be true in building a business that you can work *on* rather than a job that you work *in* with a boss you do not like even though you see that person's face in the mirror every morning.

Each step is broken down into subsequent modules and if implemented will begin to provide you with margin in your time and income, giving you freedom to live out your skillset and giftedness in powerful ways. Beware. If implemented, the discovery you are about to walk through will bring exciting results and will also require increased responsibility with those results. The responsibility is worth it. Let's dive into step one of your Four Steps to Business Freedom.

Step One: Get Clarity

Get Clarity about Your Future (Vision)

The world of a contractor is generally straightforward: bid a project, win or lose the bid, invoice, complete the work, argue with the general contractor or customer along the way, and collect payment (sometimes).

The contractor world is a world addicted to chaos.

Bret wanted to turn the world of heavy equipment operation and land excavation on its head, so he made a move. He was unclear about where he was headed in his business and what he wanted to see accomplished. Bret had a picture in his mind but not on paper, so his employees, vendors, customers, and stakeholders were not able to own it. He drafted a detailed snapshot of the future of his business, a vision story.

- What do I want my family and my freedom to look like? (A powerful question that MUST be answered but often gets overlooked)
- What do I want my financials to look like? Revenues, expenses, margins?
- What types of services do I want to offer?
- What type of personnel do I need to offer those services and get to those target financials, and what type of culture do I want to build?
- What is the ideal customer do I want to serve?

Bret had the answers to these questions in his mind. But Bret was in silent chaos with ideas screaming in his head. He had not placed them in a visual logical flow that would spark continual review and, most importantly, allow Bret and the Barnhart Excavating team to implement them effectively.

Bret answered the questions one by one.

"By 2020, I see us . . ."

This is what Bret put on the first line of each page he wrote. After 45 minutes, a document emerged. It looked like a typical business document, but Bret knew it was more than that. Bret realized he was literally shaping and crafting the future of his family, his team, and the people he would serve.

Bret finally had a place to go when he needed to make tough decisions on whom to recruit, whom to serve, how to serve, what equipment to purchase and sell, and which locations were a fit and which were not. Instead of allowing chaos to determine the next decisions, he created a predictable document that served as home base, as an anchor.

When boating in the rivers of South Carolina's Lowcountry, it is not possible to turn the boats off and stay in one place. The tides are either coming in, or they are going out. If you want to boat in these rivers, you better have a depth finder, and you should carry an anchor.

When the boat silences, the anchor drops and eventually catches on the floor of the river. The line quietly snaps to let you know the anchor has caught.

Just because your anchor is holding you in one general place does not mean that it prevents the boat from floating in a radius equal to the amount of rope that stretches between the boat and the anchor. The tides are constantly moving, so the boat revolves around the anchor. Although the boat is free to float, the anchor ensures you stay in one small area.

Bret finally had the anchor of a vision story in the water for the boat of his business to be able to float around. While the tides of business (customers, billing, equipment maintenance, employee reviews, market volatility, leasing, purchasing, team meetings, etc.) were ripping inland, Bret's boat was able to remain in stable in one place and simply rise with the tide.

Bret was able to make decisions with an end in mind. Reactions to situations were becoming less common in the business, and Bret was beginning to breed a sense of consistency, thoughtfulness, intentionality, and clarity.

Bret realized through this process that clarity even with disagreement drives continuity in decision-making. The Barnhart Excavating team was being exposed to this new detailed vision of the future in the context of team meetings and intentional conversation that helped progress the business.

Business progresses at massive speed and scale, and there are certain pillars that have been steady since the foundation of the world.

Vision was a part of history before humans existed. The world was formed from something that was "formless and void," and that transformation hinged on a vision.

Modern Israel became a nation in 1948, but the people of Israel were a nation thousands of years ago. How did Israel get started? Abraham had a vision from God, who said, "Go to a land I will show you . . . and I will make you a great nation" (Genesis 12). This nation continues to exist in part due to a foundation built on a solid vision.

- Through vision, nation-states emerge.
- Through vision, husbands and wives grow and
  lead families.
- Through vision, planners and developers build a city.
- Through vision, athletic teams chase championships.

- Through vision, we have technology doubling each year or two since the beginning of the twenty-first century.
- Through vision, crooked leaders mislead and influence otherwise decent people to conduct indecent campaigns against others.
- Through vision, we have the opportunity to see things as we have never seen them, and to experience realities that were never before available.

The Wright brothers had a vision, and today, we are able to fly around the world and into outer space. Karl Benz had a vision, and today, we are all driving around in the automobile. Leonardo Da Vinci had vision fleshed out in thousands of pages of notes, sketches, and diagrams.

This book is a direct result of my vision to help liberate you from the chaos of working in your business and help get your life back as a small-business owner. I saw the big picture of this book in my mind and on one sheet of paper before I began writing the first word.

You have a desire to see your life and your business develop into something that will bring life and value to someone. If you build your business without a vision, you are a boat floating out in the open ocean without an anchor, GPS, or a compass. Eventually, you will run out of gas.

Make a different choice.

Draw a line in the sand.

Choose now to take action and develop a vision that will be a clarifying reality for the stakeholders in your life. If you are a homebuilder who builds homes at $250k and your vision calls for you to begin building homes $500k and above, your suppliers and subcontractors need to know that!

If your vision calls for you to make a transition in your business, your employees need to know.

Once you have a vision, you must communicate that vision (more on that later). For now, decide that you will describe the detailed picture of what you see in the months and years to come.

You have a gift, and we are waiting for your vision so we can decide if we want to go on the journey with you!

How to Build a Vision

You know you need a vision, but how in the world do you stop long enough to articulate what you see? How do you even know what you see? Is it a real picture or just some crazy image in your head that would freak others out?

You respond in frustration, "But we've done these before, and the documents just sit in a really expensive binder on a really expensive shelf and gather cheap dust."

You are right. An unimplemented vision does just that!

Joe Calloway, author of *Magnetic*, relays one of my favorite sayings: "Vision without implementation is hallucination!"

If vision has brought to life all of these great realities of human existence, then I can make an argument that failing to articulate your vision is to neglect the world of something great that we could otherwise experience.

It is misguided to think that vision is only reserved for elite intellectuals. Vision is available to everyone from corporate suites to plastic folding garage tables. Vision is available to all and discriminates against none.

The only holdup to a powerful vision is a lack of implementation, and now there is no excuse for that, either, because I am going to walk you step by step through exactly how to craft a vision for your business (**check out CreateAFamilyVision. com** to create a Vision for your family).

I would like to extend my gratitude to . . .

- Elon Musk for taking your vision of a rocket, a long-range electric automobile, and a scalable solar factory and bringing it to life.
- Steve Jobs for taking your vision of an incredible suite of digital game-changers and bringing them to life.
- Truett Cathy for taking your vision of the chicken sandwich (BRILLIANT!) and bringing it to life.
- Dallas Willard for taking your vision of God's Word translated into common language and bringing it to books and speeches.

- The cheese shop owner in the Olta Arno district of Florence for your vision of traveling the world to study the art and science of cheese making.
- The traveler who saw an empty piano at gate A11 in the Bergamo airport and had the vision to begin playing Ed Sheeran tunes, which cut the anxiety of flying for the rest of us.
- One of my mentors, the late Dr. Mike Barnett, for taking your vision of sharing what vision actually is with a naive twenty-three-year-old theology student.

If you were to pause and take a look around, you would see that you are surrounded by products, services, and landscapes that are all a result of vision. Where there is vision, we thrive. Where there is no vision, we die (Prov. 29:18).

A vision is what you see. Vision is a snapshot with image-based words and phrases that describe in great detail exactly what you see in a defined period of time from now. Vision is a long-range telescope in the myopic world of small-business chaos.

Here are four tools that you will need in order to create your vision and conquer chaos.

First, you need time and space.

A campaign has been underway since the onset of widespread digitization and computational opportunity that has encouraged us to "multitask." But researcher Sherry Turkle author of *Reclaiming Conversations* notes that we should abandon multitasking because *"it is neither efficient nor conducive to empathy" and instead focus on "unitasking."* Do one thing at a time.

Give yourself a genuine gift. Find a quiet space, and set aside one hour with your phone in another room in " airplane mode" so no one can interrupt.

I know. Your mind will scream in opposition. Punch your mind in the face (metaphorically of course). Tell it to settle down, and you will deal with it later. I can see another perspective that your mind cannot, and I promise you the world will continue unabated while your phone is silent for one hour as you write out your vision. It will have a lifelong impact!

Recently, a gathering of broker/owner residential property managers asked if I would speak at their annual conference. I spoke about the slowness of wisdom and the value of silence and solitude *in a hotel ballroom in Las Vegas* (The Mirage) with 700 people filling the room. Irony was everywhere. Two things left me beaming after the talk. First, I asked everyone to put their phones on airplane mode, and most of them seemed to do it as indicated by their eye contact throughout. Second, I had the entire room go completely silent for forty seconds. For forty seconds, I gave each attendee likely the only quiet they would experience during their waking hours while in Vegas. It felt like an eternity.

This may have been the first time many of these people had forty seconds of intentional time being still, focused, and quiet. They may not have thought it was possible to experience that type of stillness, focus, and quiet. You may not think it is possible, but it is possible. So, decide right now.

Do you choose the unfulfilling, momentary candy of the phone and social media, or the game-changing, revolution breeding, life-altering space that good vision demands?

Choose vision!

Set a time in your calendar right now.

Seriously, right now.

Go do it.

Right. Now.

Second, you need an accessible platform.

You need a stage you can display this performance on. You need a stage whereby your vision can find a home, a hub, a central place to be reviewed on a regular basis. For some, this is a blog. For others, it is a podcast. Options continue to arise, but the truth remains: you must have a platform where your audience can gather to see you.

While I am looking more and more to limit the access that things have in my life, our vision is something that I want access to at any given moment. Proliferation is preferred in access to your vision instead of sanctions and limitations.

You need your vision accessible anytime, anywhere so that you can be reminded of it and run!

At the time of this writing, the tech revolution has provided you and me with a real gift. It is a gift without a direct cash expense, completely free up to 15GB (go to **letyourbusinessburn.com** as I walk you thru how to set up your own free account). Do not be fooled, there is a tradeoff for the gift that Google has provided through Google Drive; your information in exchange for their free tools. Scott Galloway's insightful book *The Four* will walk you through a different perspective these companies.

Remember when you had to pay hundreds of dollars for the Microsoft suite of products to run your office? New tech companies have remade those into a cloud-based studio that double as fancy digital filing cabinets. Think about it: you need a filing cabinet *and* you need a studio to create. Cloud-based platforms have both.

The Business On Purpose vision (see our public vision at **letyourbusinessburn.com**) is written on a Google Doc so we can get access to it whether we are at home, in France, on a cliff in Utah, or in Nigeria online or offline. I am writing this entire book on a Google Doc (currently on a plane just over the southern tip of Greenland, which is actually not green). Regardless of what you use, make sure the place that are choosing to document your vision is a place you can regularly have access to.

You may say, "Well, my grandfather did not have all these things, and he is just fine!" Well, your grandfather was not having to process 20,000 years of progress a single century either. He could not drive a car 400 miles on electricity alone, had really bad breath, and his barber made his ear bleed every time he cut his hair. I am sure Peepaw (a southern grandfather) is cool, but stop thinking he was living the dream.

The world is inherently more complicated and noise-filled today than when Peepaw was in his heyday. Glean from the good ole days what you can; now it is time to come on in and leverage the technology that is here and what is coming tomorrow with one word of caution—*you decide to own the technology and not let the technology own you.*

What platform will you use to write out your vision? Go ahead and create that document and title it The (Company) Vision. We'll get into what you'll put into that document.

Third, you need detailed categories.
Vision statements are okay but are necessarily deficient in fully capturing what you see down the road because they are not built with thought-out dreams.

Imagine a small landscaping company that is currently generating $1.2 million in annual revenue and wishes to grow to $1.2 billion in annual revenue in two years. The simple vision statement might declare that they see themselves as a $1.2 billion company in two years. The owner has clearly not given thought on what it would feasibly take (the work, the manpower, the equipment, the processes, and the capital) to build that type of operation that fast.

Though it sounds nice and aggressive, that kind of vision is not realistic and can lead to bad stewardship of your life and resources.

You retort, wild eyed, "What about Facebook and Airbnb that in just a few years are worth billions?"

Every rule has an exception, and even those exceptions have backstories.

Fourth, you need your ideas.

Before a couple has a child, they naturally begin thinking, "I hope my child will grow to . . ." Parents have quiet expectations that they revisit sporadically in the midst of the chaos of raising a family. Thoughts like, "I hope she . . ." and "I really want him to learn _____ so he can_____ when he grows up." The children turn nine, and the mom and dad hope they have not ruined the kids. The children turn fifteen, and the parents think, "Certainly I have screwed this whole thing up."

We have ideas for our children—what they will name their kids, where they will work, and how they will raise their own family. Our kids subconsciously take our ideas with them and many times will settle for our ideas for them rather than the ideas that God has uniquely placed inside them.

A massive challenge in parenting is reserving our own preference and replacing it with stewarding giftedness.

As you prepare to write out *your* vision, please remember this important point . . .

It is **your** vision.

Influences from others are natural and will be inherent, but just because your mom always thought you would be great working with geriatric patients does not mean that her hope for you should make your final vision (unless *you* see yourself working with geriatric patients).

The Seven Vision Categories

Having categories in place that guide your written vision will also help you think methodically through the implications of the ultimate vision. There are the seven categories that we have found to be essential in crafting a powerful and thoughtful vision. This seven-category vision is chaos' greatest fear.

Term: When you look out into the future, how many months or years will it take to get to the picture that you see? There is really no magic to this. Just pick a date that seems reasonable to the powerful vision you see.

There have been visions historically that are as brief as a few months (Nehemiah), mid-term such as six years (Daniel 8:26), and as long as generations (Genesis 12:1–2).

My Coach's Tip: I have found a sweet spot for small-business owners to draft a vision that is between 18 months and 6 years . . . typically 3 years.

Family/Freedom: "I wish I would have spent *less* quality time with my family," said no one ever. The reason we start small businesses is, in large part, both the opportunity to have margin and freedom to spend with people we love while offering a powerful service to our community.

The first category that you will want to give great attention and detail to is what you see for your family. Do you want to travel together, spend more time building Legos®, going to events, climbing trees, or having dinner together every night? What about go-karts and mini-bikes? (Yes, we have a mini-bike. Go to **letyourbusinessburn.com/mini** to see my skills.) What do you really see? This is your time to get it all out now! This is your chance to plant a stake in the ground for your family by declaring that chaos will not rule the days in your home.

Example: I see our family eating dinner together four nights per week around a dinner table somewhere.

Example: I see myself taking Ashley for a weekend getaway four times per year.

Financials: "It's not about the money for me." If I had a quarter for every time that I have heard that as a business coach! The financial books will not keep themselves, and profits, in

33

my experience, do not automatically deposit themselves into a special account that pile up now for magical distribution when you decide to stop working.

In short, stop guessing, and start being intentional around what you really see. Mike Michalowicz has propelled a helpful shift in practical business accounting that encourages a "Profit First" mindset taking revenue and shoveling the profit margin, owner's pay, and tax money into separate accounts before paying all other expenses.

There is one major problem with this mindset.

Most businesses have no idea what their profit could be, should be, and currently is. Certainly there are industry standards that you can measure against (the Profit First Instant Assessment can help you with that). Regardless, a powerfully simple first question to ask is, "In real dollars (or your local currency), what do I want my net profit to be? How much money do I want to have in the bank that I can personally draw from?"

Your net profit will tell you how much revenue you will need to generate once you factor in your expenses. This will definitely take the time and space that you have already laid out.

In full candor, I loathe the financial stuff too, so you are not alone. Would I rather jam my eyes out with a hot poker than do the books? Yep. But I know that will not get me to my vision, and my eyes will hurt! Chaos loves disrupting your life with the instrument of money.

My Coach's Tip: At least try to fill in these three data points: a) Desired (be realistic) Real Profit (after everything is paid out including taxes), b) Expenses, c) Total Revenue.

Product/Service: I remember the first time I laid eyes on a Snuggie®. You know, that bizarrely wearable blanket. Why didn't I think of that? As of 2015, it has reportedly sold more than a half a *BILLION* dollars.

The Snuggie® is a simple concept that appeals to a variety of people both as an everyday product and as a gag-party novelty. You cannot help but chuckle when you open the gift package and see that goofy actor on the front of the box smiling like the product has brought home a feeling of temporary significance and happiness.

I have never owned nor worn a Snuggie®, so what do I know? Maybe the goofy smile is real! Snuggie® is doing something right. What is it? They have found something that the market wants for a variety of reasons, and they are bringing it to the people reliably, affordably, and consistently.

This may be the quirkiest statement of this book: *You have a Snuggie® inside of you as well!*

You have a product and/or service that the market wants, and it is up to you to define it.

Allen Ward is a gifted and brilliant civil engineer in the Lowcountry of South Carolina. Allen is a born and bred South Carolinian with a slow, hospitable welcome and a mind for business. Allen's orange-biased red hair serves as a constant display of passion for the Clemson Tigers, my arch nemesis being a South Carolina Gamecock.

Allen has built a business that offers a service that has helped to progress and change the entire geographical face of a region. Before a building goes up or a road goes down, Allen and his team at Ward Edwards Engineering make sure it fits with the landscape, the environment, and vital community infrastructure systems such as transportation, water, sewer, stormwater, telecommunications, and power. As a business, Ward Edwards Engineering has articulated clearly what services they provide and *which services they do not provide.*

We were talking one day in the Ward Edwards conference room when I told Allen that he has a real "narrow brilliance." A light bulb came on for both of us when I said it; it was an aha. I have come to define "narrow brilliance" as something that God has given you a unique capability, expertise, and passion to do that he has not given to most.

Allen could fly a plane (he has a private pilot's license), run a sports franchise, or run a landscape company. Allen could do a lot of things, but his narrow brilliance is the ability to craft healthy community through the utility of civil engineering.

As the father of two girls, Allen also owns a "Snuggie®," and he's not afraid to use it.

What are you better at than 95% of your friends? What is your narrow brilliance? Identify the products and/or services that you either currently offer or wish to offer in the future.

Working with a concrete contractor, Garett Harvey had his head down as a business owner and yet wanted to push his business beyond the standard gruff concrete contractor setup. Writing out the vision, he was able to articulate an area within his expertise that required a certain peculiarity that kept many other contractors from entering his industry market.

Tabby concrete is a unique blend of concrete and oyster shells that cross-dissolves the structural hardscape of the South Carolina Lowcountry into the natural landscape that many of us have the privilege of breathing in each day. Tabby is not easy for most contractors. Pouring and setting Tabby is a narrow brilliance that Garett and his team have. It translates into a marketable confidence that allows thousands of Lowcountry residents to build a structural legacy in a classic style.

What is your Tabby? What is your Snuggie®?

What product or service is within your narrow brilliance? Chaos has a hard time distracting you or your team when you have articulated your product. You know what to say yes to, and you know where to direct your "Enlightened No" (a great phrase I learned from Gay Hendricks' book *The Big Leap*). Hendricks says, "You produce an Enlightened No when you turn down something that doesn't fit into your Zone of Genius."

Your product should be squarely within your "Zone of Genius."

Personnel: "If it were not for the employees, I would *love* my business," said a client of mine with a forced smile. Informally, as I have polled my clients, the number-one headache typically has to do with employees.

As we were placing the finishing touches on a series of job roles for a small construction firm, my heroic client simply said, "Why can't they just do what seems so common sense?" Do not ever forget this: *what is common to you is not necessarily common to everyone else.*

Justine has been keeping books for small- to medium-sized homebuilding companies for the past 30 years. She has lived a life of data entry, payables, receivables, change orders, rebates, and collections. Every Tuesday, she trudges through payroll, and every Wednesday, she coordinates all of the subcontractor paperwork.

After three decades, Justine is finally going to retire to a life of Bunko groups, volunteering at the local Boys & Girls Club, and traveling to visit grandkids. No longer will she sit at a desk and daydream about new techniques for ledger adjustments. She will be locked in on little people daydreaming about rocket ships and American Girl dolls instead.

There's just one problem: you own the business that Justine works for, and you have to figure out a plan to replace of her talent, insight, and skill set. You come to a stark realization of the powerful truth I mentioned earlier; *what is common to you* (or Justine) *is not necessarily common to everyone else.* You could find someone with 20 years of bookkeeping talent, but how they do the books is like night and day. What is common to Justine is simply not common to the new guy.

The benefit derived from having employees is in direct proportion to the effort that you the business owner will commit to training and investing in each of your team members. We have found that the success of the employee has more to do with the engagement and training that the business owner is willing to invest.

The personnel issue will drive a business owner back to life as an employee faster than any other small-business issue. It is a massive door for chaos to enter.

When articulating your vision story, you can use a simple formula for determining the number of employees that you will need. Go back to your family/freedom category. To get to your family/freedom goals, you will need to meet your financial goals. To meet your financial goals, you will have to sell _____ number of products/services. To sell that prescribed number of products/services, you will need a team composed of _____. To compensate that team, you will need to pay them _____.

Match it up with your financial category and there you go. If you do not like the layout and number of that team, then you may need to go back and adjust the prior vision elements to match. It all connects!

Client Type: A stark, rough, and city-originated business-man transplanted to a quirky little area in this Southern rich coastal bluff town in hopes of cashing in on the recent growth of the area by building a new location for a hospitality business. As the build out continued, he began engaging in professional design services, and he met the principal of the design firm.

The design of the beautiful structure took shape, and the transplanted businessman proved himself to be more and more agitated by the process because he considered it to be too detailed and lengthy for the type of structure he wanted to establish. A couple of months went by, the design progressed, and the invoices either returned to the firm contested or went unpaid. This was turning into a nightmare client for this highly regarded small architecture firm.

The principal of the firm was caught in a sticky situation: "We needed the work, but this guy is a disaster!"

When you are building a small business from the ground up and desperate for revenue and cash flow, every potential client looks like a dream come true, and yet some really do turn out to be a chaos-inducing nightmare.

When preparing for a promotional campaign, marketing gurus ask clients, "Who is your avatar?" What is the specific type of person and/or business that you wish to work with? What is the profile of a person and/or business that you absolutely *do not* wish to work with?

A recent client has spent three decades designing outdoor kitchens and spaces for clients. He finally declared, "I am tired of working with 'do it yourselfers' who have a bad back; they nickel and dime and see little value in our professional insight and peculiarities!"

Did you know that you can *choose* the type of person that you would like to serve? Yes, you can actually say no to working with chaos-loving clients.

Are you going to hit it every time? Of course not. After you articulate your ideal client type, your paths will begin to subtly cross as if they opened the front door and said, "I have been waiting for you to knock!"

Go ahead and write it out. Who is your ideal client? What are their habits, tendencies, size, background, scope, hopes, and dreams? Write it out so you and those you lead and serve will have great clarity and so *those who read it may run* and conquer the chaos.

Culture: "Um, Muhammed, do you know where we are going?" This is what I asked my friend when we trekked deep into the Nigerian bush. We had worked with our friends in rural parts of Nigeria, but I was nervous about how deep we were going.

We had traveled well off the Federal Highway into the hinterlands of the bush, and we had forayed into villages with families who had never seen a white person before. Every Nigerian we passed would gaze at us as if we were the featured talking gorilla at the local zoo. I guess we returned the same awed looks to them.

After we arrived at our camp, we walked into an area filled with women and children, huts, small cooking fires, and the smell of aromatic cuisine, the likes of which have been prepared in a place like this for centuries. Solomon's words, "there is nothing new under the sun," resonated with me in a powerful way in this camp. Except for the occasional ring of a QWERTY cell phone and the glow of a battery-powered LED flashlight, it felt as if we had caught a time-traveling passenger train back to the 1700s.

Tribal marks, naked babies, livestock, and feeding troughs made for a set that not even Disney could have pulled off. Muhammed took off to enter camp in a nomadic stride coming from the edge of the cleared ground toward its center. Emerging out of a dark shadow solemnly resting under a tree sat an aged man wearing the appearance of Islamic clothing. Muhammed hit the ground, prostrate, as they began to mumble back and forth.

"Aku a nani." Muhammed greeted this elder, offering

him polite questions on the pleasantries of how his cows, his children, his wives, and his family were doing. After a few minutes of this rhythmic back and forth, Muhammed finally got up, looked at us appearing as if we had just seen a ghost, and simply smiled and said, "This is Al Hajji Salo. He greets you."

Without missing a beat, we greeted him. "Haloooo, nize tu seeee uuuu, tank uuuuu," as if changing the pronunciation and cadence of our English language would somehow allow his ears to magically translate into his native Fulfulde language. He smiled graciously not understanding what we are saying short of Muhammed providing humorous translation.

While in Nigeria, we had often laughed at the thousands of ways we looked out of place in this culture not our own, even though we loved it. While business culture differs from anthropological culture, businesses do have a culture. The good news is you can have a quicker impact on your business culture. Some people will fit with your language and customs; some will not. Better to write out the vision of what you see and create the culture of your business now so that sothers will appreciate it for what it is, embrace it, and move the business forward.

How do days in the office or meetings flow? Is yours a business that smiles, plays, pushes, runs, jogs, sits, listens, tells? How do your team members interact? How does the leadership see the team and vice versa? Does your business have art and color or straight lines and grays?

Using image-based words will allow others to see if yours is a business they want to be a part of. It will also allow you to see if this is a business you want to lead. Jim Mattei, the man who helped to create the Checker's Hamburger Franchise, said simply of culture, "If you don't get it right, everything else breaks down."

If you do not articulate culture, chaos will be your default.

Once you have spent time thoughtfully thinking through the details of your vision story, the detailed snapshot of what the future looks like however many years from now, you become perfectly positioned to begin building a memorizable and portable version of that vision story.

Think of it as your vision story in miniature.

Welcome to your mission statement.

What Gets You
Out Of Bed On Tuesday

(Mission Statement)

"This company is unbelievable!" exclaimed Ashley. A couple of days prior to this declaration, Ashley had been on the hunt and kill for a new pair of shoes for one of our children whose foot growth was outpacing the speed of our wallet growth.

Ashley had heard of an online superstore where she could pick up the right pair of shoes from a massive collection in the right size for a reasonable price. The shoes arrived the day after she ordered them.

The shoes were too small.

Ashley submitted the online return request and the new shoe order.

The correctly sized shoes arrived the next day before we had the chance to send the old shoes back. Better yet, there was no extra charge either way.

Imagine that. Typically, if you order the wrong item, a company requires a shipping fee, an affidavit demonstrating truthfulness, a credit check, background check, a visit to an offshore consulate office for lightning-speed fingerprinting,

and a blank money order made out to the company directly .
Or something close to that.

"Who is this company?" I asked in complete shoe-amazement.

Zappos.

Being a business enthusiast and constantly fascinated
with the novelty of how businesses operate, I researched
Zappos and came across the mission that gets them out of
bed every morning.

You would think that the mission of Zappos is simply
"to sell great shoes."

No.

Zappos team members get out of bed for this singular
purpose: "to provide the best customer service possible!"[1]

A mission statement is a succinct sentence describing
what drives you out of bed in the morning. Some might refer
to the mission statement as a purpose statement. The mission statement is both tied to and yet structurally different
from your vision story. Your mission statement emerges from
your vision story to lay the foundation for your life and the
lives of the people around you to be changed forever.

For years, the vision statement and the mission statement
have looked similar. They were perceived as fraternal twins—
different enough for people to know there was a difference
and yet similar enough to not know what that difference is.

Seeing a lack in the substance that a vision statement

was offering in light of the mission statement, we moved our clients toward the broader and more detailed vision story. The thoughtful, detailed vision story provides a clear difference and opportunity for the power of the mission statement to blaze forward while offering a succinct, wireless, portable, and memorizable nugget that allows the broader vision story to be seen from a distance.

The detailed vision story is now highlighted and promoted by the brief and portable mission statement.

I was recently asked on Facebook, "Is the mission statement dead?"

My response, "YES, BAD mission statements are dead!"

Clichéd mission statements are dead.

Vanilla mission statements are dead.

Impotent mission statements are . . . dead.

Maybe now is time to launch the "Make the Mission Statement Great Again" campaign. It worked for the 2016 President-elect Donald Trump, so maybe it will resurrect the focus that people and businesses should be placing on the priority of rightly placed, well-articulated mission.

It is hard to argue with a mission statement that moves, compels, gives insight, and inspires. It is even more challenging to defeat the opposition when they are rallied around that simple mission.

When chaos is confronted with a small business armed and actively using their mission statement, chaos will lose.

How about these mission statements directly from Jesus Christ, arguably the most mission-centric man in human history?

- *I came to* seek and save the lost.
- *I came to* set the captives free.
- *I came to* give sight to the blind.
- *I came to* give life and give it overflowing.

Those are statements of mission. Mission is "an important assignment, a calling."[2]

So, what is the anatomy of a good mission statement that has meaningful utility beyond a simple tagline and will be powerful ammunition to conquer chaos? There are three primary structure points that make up the anatomy of a mission statement.

Memorizable

Confession time. When I scroll a business website (small or large), I am always curious about where I can find what drives them out of bed in the morning. If I am able to find a mission statement, it is typically a paragraph or more of nice hopes that are typically dressed in cliché. "A mind is a terrible thing to waste." Yes, it is.

I am sure some brilliant neuroscientist has already uncovered that we have an affinity to remember short, pithy statements or phrases. Fill in the gap of each company's tagline or name.

1. Nike
2. Wendy's Hamburgers
3. Like a good neighbor
4. Save 15% in 15 minutes
5. Got _ _ _ _?
6. There are some things money cannot buy, for everything else there is

Answer Key:

1. Just Do It.
2. Where's the Beef?
3. State Farm is there.
4. Geico
5. Milk
6. Master Card

As of this writing, Donald J. Trump has been elected as the President of the United States of America. Regardless of political bias and affiliation, ask yourself this question: What was the phrase that the Hillary Clinton campaign leveraged throughout her Presidential campaign?

Do you know it?

Most do not. Friends of mine close to the campaign told me the campaign slogan was "I'm With Her."

Can you remember Donald Trump's?

"Make America Great Again."

I am not saying that Trump only won because of a memorizable campaign slogan. But he had one, and the Clinton campaign did not. If given the choice, I would take a memorizable mission that people can remember and rally around.

Wireless and Portable

Years ago, the satellite revolution ushered in an era of portable communications that altered technology. Satellites were used to provide internet to rural areas. Not until things became more wireless, decentralized, and portable did the need arise for greater capacity in handling novel technologies. New means and methods of travel and exploration have been possible due to wireless and portable communication.

You want your mission to be wireless and portable. You want it to have the launching, orbiting, and enduring power of a satellite that everyone can gain access to, which can lead to the nimble outmaneuvering of chaos.

Having a mission statement that is wireless and portable means it can stand alone. Your mission statement will have enough content to reveal *why* you do what you do. Simon Sinek, author of *Start With Why*, has done a brilliant job of resurrecting the historical idea of mission in the modern society. He wrote, "There are only two ways to influence human behavior: you can manipulate it, or you can inspire it." A portable and wireless mission statement brings an awe and inspiration that influences the right people to stop and take note. Chaos included.

"Leadership is the ability to rally people not for a single event, but for years," says Sinek. The most vocal, sustainable, and simplest rallying tool a business owner has is a wireless and portable mission statement.

Potent

Living the majority of my life in the Southern United States has "afforded" me an awareness of what the bootleggers aptly named "mountain dew" or "white lightning."

My college roommate and I had an opportunity to intern during summers at a super speedway in the mecca of stock car racing during its heyday, challenging accents, and a good ole boy network that spanned generations. Each year the speedway hosted the longest race in stock car racing, a grueling 600 miles in circles.

The grind was not merely reserved for the drivers and their crews, but for the fans and the thousands of support workers, ticket takers, parking attendants, concession staff, and executive level leadership. While my roommate and I were not earning executive level pay or making executive level decisions, we had access to all of the executive level offices and meetings. We were two interns just trying the learn the ropes!

When the race was over that year, we found ourselves sitting with the president of the speedway, a few key staff, and a couple of NFL football players who were stars for the local franchise team.

As the late night wore on into the early hours of the morning, the speedway owner pulled out a ratty box that I had seen earlier in the week while tending to my usual intern duties.

I had been sitting at the desk of the assistant to the president earlier in the week when Mountain Man came gliding into the room with "Papaw Blue" boot-cut jeans, worn mountain-cowboy boots, and signature wafting silver hair enhanced by a beautiful pair of stylish mutton chops framing each side of his leathery face.

Mountain Man did not acknowledge me; he just glided straight into the president's office with a cocked grin and jars full of moonshine.

Moonshine has never been my thing. Channeling my inner chemist, it fascinates me how the 'shine is made, though. In short, you fill a large barrel with a mash substance and send liquid through a series of chemical breakdowns, purification, and condensation. Out of that massive drum of mash comes a small, potent drop.

BOOM!

52

An average beer holds around 4–5% alcohol in total volume.

An average glass of wine holds around 10–12% alcohol in total volume.

An average shot of spirit holds around 40% alcohol in total volume.

Then there is moonshine, some varieties carrying up to 75% alcohol by volume.

It is common knowledge that it does not take much to light a person up.

Your mission statement will be a potent drop of "white lightning" leaving an impact on the people who ingest it!

Leave the hearer asking, "How?"

As Simon Sinek says, "People do not buy *what* you do, they buy *why* you do it. A failure to communicate *why* creates nothing but stress or doubt."

If your *why* interests me enough, do not worry, I will ask you the *what* later when we are actually doing business together. I do not care as much about *how* Mitch Dyess and the team at Dyess Heating and Air fix my air conditioning unit, but that our unit blows cold air in the dead of summer and that they are courteous and kind!

It happens all of the time: you walk into the party, and someone asks you what you do.

Your first response usually revolves around facts and

LET YOUR BUSINESS BURN

statistics, the "doing" part of work. You respond, "I run a bookkeeping firm that focuses on accounts payable, accounts receivables, general ledgers, payroll, account management, receipt and expense management, forecasting, blah, blah, blah."

"We work with twenty-seven clients that have total revenues between $300k to $5M annually."

Facts and statistics.

What if you responded this way instead? "We eliminate financial headaches so small-business owners can build real profit!"

Whoa! Sign me up!

A great "why" leaves the hearer nowhere else to turn but to be compelled to ask, "How?"

Your mission statement is your "why." It is the reason you got out of bed this morning.

Make it compelling. Make it thoughtful, insightful, and peculiar.

Your mission is not to wake up and "become the world's leading blah blah blah."

Be compelling. What is *your* narrow brilliance? What drives *you* out of bed?

Brennan Manning, author of the *Ragamuffin Gospel*, speaking at a Cru Convention in the '90s at Colorado State University, asked a question that has hovered over me since then: "What makes you cry?"

YES!

What makes you cry? What moves you? What brings you irrational joy when you are around it?

For me, I LOVE liberating small-businesss owners from the chaos of working in their business. It makes me giddy like a child when one of our heroic small-businesss owners has a breakthrough.

It has caused me to cry, to scream, to laugh (a real belly laugh!), and to cheer when we see that liberation.

How You Build Your Mission Statement

How do you get to a portable, memorizable, and potent mission statement that you can carry around in your pocket and use all of the time?

1. Go back to your vision story.
2. Highlight up to forty words that stick out to you as keywords from your vision story (verbs, adjectives, etc.).
3. Select your top fourteen words from the ones that you have highlighted, and write them down in a list.
4. From that list, compile different sentences together that will eventually form a mission. Each sentence must be less than fifteen words and must be memorizable!
5. Start each sentence with "We exist to . . ."

For instance, if you are a bookkeeping firm and some of your keywords are:

Processed	Edgy	Clutch
Laughter	Really smart	Freedom

then your sentence ideas may look something like this:

We exist to turn imprisoned entrepreneurs into clutch performers.
We exist to replace business misery with laughter and freedom.
We exist to free smart entrepreneurs from last-minute frustrations and into clutch performance.
We exist to get business owners away from debits and credits and into laughter and freedom! (Notice the words of double meaning = "debits and credits.")

I intentionally did not spend much time on these. These are not words from clients that I have worked with in the past. I came up with these words off the top of my head and created some sentences that are more compelling than the typical "We exist to be the best ACME company providing customer service and products for human beings."

Your mission is not meant to be magical or turn the world on its axis; just make it interesting, compelling, and uniquely you!

Just like anything else, it is going to take time to develop and build. I suggest following Cal Newport's best practices that he discusses in his groundbreaking book, *Deep Work*. He defines deep work as "professional activities performed in a state of distraction-free concentration that push your cognitive capabilities to their limit. These efforts create new value, improve your skill, and are hard to replicate."

Developing your mission, your *why*, is a professional activity and *must* be handled as such. You want to stay distracted and chaotic? Then resist the deep work and settle for scrolling Facebook and eating digital candy!

Earlier we built out your vision story, the detailed snapshot of what you want the future of your business to look like. Let's call that your *destination*.

Your mission, in this metaphor is the car you drive to get to your destination. (I love metaphors so much that my wife bought me a book called *Metaphors Be With You!* I am a geek like that.)

My family has a fleet of "vintage" cars. The one that I currently drive is a 2002 Nissan Xterra with 212,000 miles on it. We are told it is not nice to profile people, and yet it is hard not to when you see what they drive. If I told you that I drove the latest Mercedes S63 AMG (retail price of $144,500USD currently,) you would probably have a different thought about me in contrast to my vintage Nissan.

The mission—the car you drive to get to your next destination—tells us more than you think!

Why did I choose the Nissan Xterra over the Mercedes?

How to Make Unemotional, Thoughtful Decisions That People Like! (Values)

Unique Core Values

Your vision story is a detailed snapshot of the future of your business, and your mission is what gets you out of bed every morning (or the car you drive to get to your vision). There is still a massive component missing within the foundation of the business that you are building!

One reason so many small-business owners are in chaos is because they have no standard for decision-making, no home base to return to when they have decisions to make regarding payroll, hiring, purchasing new equipment, expanding, or contracting.

Unique core values act as standards; they are an anchor. Your unique core values serve as an anchor that keeps you getting closer to your destination by empowering you to make firm decisions regardless of the weather, the tides, or the influences that will push you around. If you are anchored to your core values, then no matter how much you want to go off course, your core values will keep you tied to your vision.

We have a laugh with clients who work through the Four Steps to Business Freedom at this point when I tell them,

"You can violate your unique core values, but you need to understand where you are and how much damage it will do."

You need a set of unique core values, and I will help you build them. Before we get started it is worth answering this question; why do I call them *unique* core values?

Standard core values are things like integrity, respect, responsibility, honesty, etc. They are great words, and I hope we all have those. In fact, that is precisely the point. *I hope we all have those!* They are not *unique*.

Standard core values are values that I think should be the low barrier for starting a business. If you do not have integrity, respect, excellence, etc., I do not know that we need to be doing business together. We should *all* value those things.

Unique core values are values that are *unique*.

Unique core values are *unique* to you and are likely things that I *may not* value. It does not mean that you are wrong or that I am wrong. Instead, we just value different things.

What makes values remarkable? *Living them out.*

There is a great statement written by an old pastor writing to encourage his congregation that had been scattered all over the Middle East, Asia, and Eastern Europe. Put simply he said, "Do not merely listen to the word, and so deceive yourselves. Do what it says" (James 1:22 NIV).

Do not merely write out your vision story (your destination).

59

Do not merely write out your mission statement (what gets you out of bed).

Do not merely write out your unique core values (curbs and guideposts).

Do what they say.

One Set of Core Values Worth $4,000

A magnetic personality, and one built more for relationship than for getting down in the details and weeds of business, Ramiro Torres, the Principal Architect for TOPA Architect knew something had to change. His love for people and the clients he served has never wavered and yet running the details of his firm was getting to be overwhelming.

Ramiro is "people-first" and loves to build and sustain relationships through storytelling, laughter, and animation. His charisma is infectious and compels clients to return to the firm for projects as they appreciate the diversity of perspective that TOPA injects into each design.

After years of working from his head and foregoing thousands in revenue due to "giving work away," Ramiro decided he would enroll in the Architecture Firm Freedom Formula (AFF) based on the Four Steps to Business Freedom to foundation that I led with architectural marketing expert Enoch Sears (Business of Architecture).

As Ramiro progressed through the program with thought and diligence building the TOPA vision story, mission, unique core values, firm infrastructure (roles, meetings, accountability, etc.) and processes, he found himself in a familiar situation once again.

A client who had come to TOPA prior was returning to request a proposal for a redesign of a small facility to operate his bakery.

As TOPA went to work injecting their uniqueness into the design, the proposal was presented at $23,000 for the project. It was a thoughtful and accurate fee based on the scope of work and the uniqueness of TOPA's insight and experience.

It was time for what Ramiro had become accustomed to in his life as a firm owner. The client would present him with lower bids and ask Ramiro to come down to a lower bid ($18,000) and say, "You're my guy!"

This time, Ramiro, suspending what was natural to his personality, decided to stand firm on the unique core values that he had recently drafted through the AFF program. He kindly and gently explained to the potential client, "Due to our core values, we have proposed this project at the scope and fee that we know it will take to get you a bakery that you are proud of!" Ramiro, for the first time, stood by his fee, because now he had something to stand on, and he knew that it would lead to a project the client would be proud of!

To Ramiro's surprise, the client actually appreciated

Ramiro's conviction and thought. He laughingly (and only partially joking) asked if Ramiro would come down to $22,000 before saying, "We have a deal."

Ramiro, spirited as always, replied, "Sure, let's get started!"

Ramiro leveraged the foundation that he built by working *on* his business to garner the fee that this particular project and his firm required. That $4,000 incidentally provided the funds to pay for most of the AFF program. In one deal! Why?

He stuck with his unique core values.

The Guts to Say "No" When "Yes" *Would* Work

Chris and his business partner Justin have built two thoughtful and service-centered businesses side by side over the past eight years in the cutthroat and volatile construction industry. It has been work and sweat from the time they hung their first shingle and signed their first contract.

For years, they winged it the best they knew. As the homebuilding business (which Chris oversees) began gaining traction, the momentum turned into notoriety and then opportunity.

Their company, Shoreline Construction, was selected to build a Southern Living model home in the most exclusive neighborhood in South Carolina (Shoreline also built the HGTV Giveaway Home for 2018). Thoughtful and timeless quality continued to sprout new opportunity that led to a day in the life of the business that Chris will never forget.

The developer of the exclusive neighborhood invited Chris and his company to collaborate on building two spec-homes (homes that offered for sale but are not yet sold to anyone, hence "speculation"). In order to come in on the multimillion-dollar deal, it would require that half of the cash be provided by Chris and his company. While they had some cash reserves, what they had was not enough to cover their portion. They needed to secure a loan from an outside investor or bank.

You may say, "What is the big deal? Home builders do it *all* the time." You are right, *most* home builders do it all the time and teeter on the fence of massive profits or potential loss and bankruptcy.

Chris and Justin are incredibly mindful of their business finances and have worked themselves into a philosophy that makes them uncomfortable with borrowing money them-selves. They are so entrenched in this idea that as we were working to develop the respective unique core values within the Four Steps to Business Freedom process for each of their businesses, the first value was "fiscal responsibility," which they defined as "no debt."

Ouch!

Here is the deal of a lifetime, almost a guaranteed slam dunk in the market they were in with the risk they would have taken. The majority of homebuilders would have jumped at the opportunity. Chris knew he had to decline, but he did not know how.

He was concerned that if he told the developer no, then very little if any work would come their way in the future. If Chris would have told him yes, he knew he was violating one of his unique core values and putting Shoreline's long-term health at risk.

After Chris and I spent some time in coaching through the dilemma, Chris landed on a brilliant and completely honorable solution that was a win-win.

When the day came, Chris met with the developer of the neighborhood armed with an idea and a piece of folded paper in his back pocket.

After the casual small talk, the developer asked the inevitable: "You ready to get started?"

Chris responded, "I'm tempted (aka Chris' emotions) to do this deal with you, but I cannot."

With a peculiar look from the developer, Chris went on to explain, "We have five unique core values within our company that we run every decision through, and as we took this opportunity through these core values, there was one in particular that we could not get past with any level of comfort."

As the developer seemed curious, Chris reached in his back pocket, unfolded the sheet of paper with five words and phrases written on it.

1. Fiscally responsible (no debt)
2. Intentional relationships
3. Quality
4. Schedule
5. Integrity (Do what is right.)

As the developer gently slid the paper toward himself, Chris explained, "We have no doubt that we can pull through this exciting project with our standards of *quality*, with a *schedule* that fits what your timeline calls for, and to *do what is right* throughout the entire project. Also, the *relationship* that we have built with you over time is intentional, so that is a check. What we cannot get around is our value of *fiscal responsibility*. Sure, there are always exceptions to the rule; this just feels like a big exception to our very important rule. So, yes, I'm tempted to do this deal with you, but my company's values prevent it."

Before the developer could say anything, Chris's DISC type "I" personality went into to full people-pleasing mode as he said, "I was scared to tell you no for fear that you would not give us another shot at working together under other circumstances, and to be honest, I am still scared you will not and . . ."

The developer politely stopped Chris with a crooked grin and said, "You have just given me all the more reason why we *should* work with you in the future!"

Not only did Chris hold to the core value of fiscally responsible but through thought and intentionality, but they also hit on their value of "intentional relationships" in how they handled the entire process.

The developer went on to work a deal with another builder with success but came back to Chris for future deals because of the foundation that his company had built on their core values.

Building Your Unique Core Values

As you have built out your vision story, in details within the seven categories that we discussed earlier, then distilled that down into a very short, portable, memorizable mission statement, it has provided you with a continual look at some words that you have found to be a great priority for you.

With this short list, you can write down some other words you consider to be a real marker for who you are. If I were to ask your friends who you are, what would they say?

I will give you some examples of what I think people would say about me.

Book nerd	Likes to laugh	New things
Frugal	Loves water	Teacher
Systems and processes	Exploring nations	Flirts with his wife

They may look like they are irrelevant to what you are building, and some will sound more "business" than others. Remember though, it's never "just business." All things integrate, and so the business you are building needs to incorporate the *unique* things that you value.

One of the things I value is being a book nerd because it leads me to read great books and meet some very cerebral people whom I can learn from and never fill this appetite I have for new things. Conversely, we have loads of clients who hate reading.

From the words you highlighted in your vision story and some of the keywords that you used for your mission statement, you should have built a decent bank of words that you can use to come up with some real *unique* core values. I recommend as few as three and no more than five core values.

Please do not gloss over that last sentence. Highlight it and dog ear this page. Seven and ten and fifteen core values do not work. You cannot memorize them.

Again, your core values need to be enough so you can make real decisions with them and not too many that you forget them because they mean nothing at all!

Take the word bank and drill it down to your top five words. These are the words that you would go to battle for. The others are good, but *these five* are the ones that you will fight and claw to keep!

Got 'em?

Okay. Now I am going to stretch you even more. The words you have chosen still may be a little cliché. Go to your web browser and pull up Thesaurus.com (God's special gift to book nerds). Type in each of the unique core value words that you have boiled down into your top five, and as you type each word into the thesaurus, see if there are some other more powerful, more descriptive synonyms of those five words that may be better descriptors of what you value than your five original words.

Sometimes there will be, and sometimes there will not, but push yourself. Your vision, mission, and values are what make up the concrete foundation of the business you are building. You are going to be using them *every single week* in your business, so do not cheat out on them!

Why the Foundation Is So Crucial

There are two diagnostic questions I ask every small-business owner I have the pleasure of talking with when they are in chaos.

1. Do you have a vision of your business *written* down in detail?
2. Can you tell me about your team meetings?

We will get to the second question later on, but for now we'll focus on question one.

Yogi Berra (it's a rule to have a Yogi quote in every book, I think) said, "If you don't know where you are going, you will get there every time!" He is right. Chaos breeds chaos.

> Where there is no vision, people become detached.
> Where there is no vision, people scatter.
> Where there is no vision, people die.

Having a business without vision (destination), mission (what gets you out of bed), and unique core values (curbs and guideposts) is like having a house with no foundation. It has nothing lasting to stand on. Sure, build away, but it will fall.

And having an articulated and well-thought-out vision, mission, and unique core values and *not* using them is like having a solid foundation and then building your house on raw ground down the street. That is just silly. Make a different choice. Make the more difficult choice in the near term that will pay overwhelming benefits in the long term.

At the end of every one-on-one coaching call and mastermind group, I have the honor of facilitating, I ask this question, "When are you going to get that done?"

Pull out your calendar right now.

When are you going to write these things out and get them to a place where they are written? Remember the two extremes.

"Write the vision down so that he may run who reads it."

(Habakkuk 2:2)

or

"Vision without implementation is hallucination."

(Joe Calloway)

Let's stop hallucinating on the drug of "We've always done it this way," or "I don't have time."

Let's do something different. Block off one uninterrupted hour on your calendar right now with zero distractions so you can begin writing out your vision using the seven categories. Then, we can rinse and repeat for the mission and values.

Now that you have step one of the Four Steps to Business Freedom under your belt and will clearly identify *where* you are going to go, you are now perfectly positioned to do what Google has been doing for the last few years and what explorers have been doing for centuries. Time to go into the map-making business.

Step Two: Designing Your Chaos-Conquering Road Maps

Maps provide us turn by turn instruction on exactly where we need to be going and how we are going to get there. Map-making is as crucial in business as it is navigation, exploration, city planning, and shipping.

I walked into Chief Doyin's office after not seeing him for about six months, and he immediately smiled and said, "Dr. David Livingstone?" Chief was making a light-hearted racial inference to the famed Scottish (hence white-skinned) explorer who left the pale racial and aggressive political climates of Western Europe and explored his way across the "dark continent" of Africa as a medically trained missionary.

We have had the opportunity to spend at least two weeks a year in Nigeria over the past ten years, and sometimes up to as much as six weeks. We began partnering with local Nigerians through various societal domains (education, business, healthcare, etc.) and coordinating a variety of faith-based opportunities and solutions for locals and for many outside the country as well.

A dear mentor of mine, Bob Roberts, taught me about a mindset that he learned from business called "glocal." It is a clear merging of two words. "Whatever you do locally, do it globally, and whatever you do globally, do it locally."

As time progressed, we developed dear friendships and relationships with our Nigerian partners, and Chief Adedoyin Bolaji definitely fits within the category.

Chief Doyin is a local statesman in a rural part of Nigeria and has been serving the town of Egbe in Kogi State his entire life, even while he lived in other cities. Inevitably, when I am in Egbe, Chief and I will find ourselves in his upstairs office, on a front porch, or somewhere in the bush discussing the history of the world through the eyes of a Nigerian man. He does most of the teaching, and I ask most of the questions.

He taught me that amidst plenty of challenges that Dr. Livingstone faced geographically, politically, emotionally, spiritually, and psychologically, he left a profound legacy that would come to have mixed reviews. The work and the walk of Dr. Livingstone provided the West with eye-opening insight into a continent that few Westerners had visited at that point. Not only was Dr. Livingstone an explorer, diplomat, tradesman, and manager, he was a map maker.

Many of his maps and diaries would serve the British

and other governments as they colonized much of the continent—again, to mixed reviews.

I love maps, seriously, almost in a weird way. Some of the art pieces hanging in our home are maps. Weird, I know. One reason I love maps is that they are a trifecta of information about the foundation of what you have read earlier in step one. Inherent in a map, you see the plotting of your destination (vision), what type of vehicle you will need to have (mission), and the boundaries of road so you do get lost (values).

The challenge to all small-business owners in drawing maps is typically taking the time to sit down and draw it out. Take this book for instance. As I mentioned earlier, the only reason this book is being written is because members of our small Business On Purpose team pushed me to set aside full days at a time (not at all back to back by the way... they do not come easy) to write.

If you want to be a map maker for your business, and you *need* to be, then it is going to require some sacrifice of time in a way *similar* to Dr. David Livingstone's sacrifice, but not to the same extent. (He sacrificed his entire life and family for that journey; it is not something I recommend).

Chaos will dominate until maps are drawn and followed. Let's design the first one now.

Road Map One:
Five Bank Accounts

Building the Profit

I must give a disclaimer that I am not a financial professional, and all training provided in this segment is provided based on experience and materials we have received from other entities. Please consult your financial and legal professional prior to making these important decisions.

Stefanie walked out of her CPA's office with a fresh copy of the net income statement for her small business. Stefanie then looked at her online bank account and asked this simple question that is asked in confusion every day of every year within the majority of small businesses and firms: "Where is the money?"

I appreciate net income statements, balance sheets, ledgers, and I absolutely LOVE a good spreadsheet . . . in almost a weird way. With all of those great tools, never in the history of business has an owner walked into a bank, handed over their net income statement, and been able to cash that piece of paper.

We own a business and are keenly aware of the priority

of having a set of healthy books, which is why we decided to outsource our bookkeeping to professionals as quickly as we could. I also know that the accounting reports are simply a barometer of the health or disease within the business and in real life rarely seem to match what is sitting in the bank account. The only thing that you can withdraw is the cash that is actually sitting in a bank account and not what is on a spreadsheet.

The goal of your five bank account road map is to set up a bank account structure and habit that will force you to be profitable immediately and to live within the means of your business while being able to take thoughtful risks.

You will know several things if you implement what we are about to show you:

You will know *exactly* how much profit you have in real Benjamins (ahem . . . hundred-dollar bills for those of you not familiar with the colloquialism).

You will know *exactly* how much you have set aside for your own compensation as the owner.

You will know *exactly* how much you have set aside for the tax man.

You will know *exactly* how much you have set aside to run your business.

Can you imagine having that level of clarity and freedom in your finances? Can you imagine the freedom you will have internally finally knowing?

The alternative is continued frustration both at work, that will follow you home and cause you to turn into a grumpy old man or woman. We already have plenty of those.

You do not have to live in the frustration. Decide right now that you are going to do something different, that you are going to take control, and *lead your business*. Decide that profit really does matter.

Why?

Because of what profit really is. Profit is not good or bad. Profit is a tool that you can leverage to *fuel your calling*. When you generate profit, it affords you the margin to push the dreams that you have. When you do not have profit, you are stuck living a life of reaction.

So, let's dive in and take control of this important part of your business. Before we get started, know this, whatever shape your business finances are in, do not beat yourself up. It is what it is, and you are here now to take action.

Everyone seems to have a "hot sports opinion" on this subject. I will share with you what is working for us. What I am about to show you has been adapted and integrated from a powerful book written by *Mike Michalowicz called "Profit First."*

Our goal is to set up a simple foundation that creates a completely new habit and freedom long term.

Let's set some context. Michalowicz introduces a concept called "Parkinson's Law." It is not related to Parkinson's disease but the idea is that "work expands so as to fill the time available for its completion."

Put another way, if you are given a small bucket of popcorn, you will eat it all.

If you are given a bucket of popcorn in a bigger size, you will eat it all.

If you only have one bank account, you will consume whatever is in it, or at least your mind will tell you that you can consume it even though you know *some* of it needs to go to taxes, savings, reinvestment, payroll, fees, etc.

This is usually where someone will pipe up and say they have it all separated in a spreadsheet! My question is how is that working for you?

What I am about to show has literally changed the outlook we have on our business. We now know exactly how much profit we have, exactly how long we can run our household if not another dime came in, exactly how much we can pay the government if not another dime came in, and exactly how long we could run the business if not another dime came in.

Exactly.

Not on some spreadsheet that does not match reality.

Let's do something different.

I want you to start by creating five strategic bank accounts. These are real accounts set up at your bank with no fees (if there are fees, find another bank).

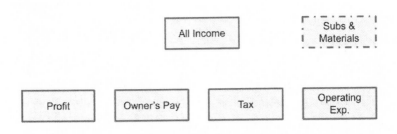

The top account will serve as a "landing account" for all generated income. With great care for naming things, we call this one your "Income account."

This can be a simple savings account that you will not need any checks or debit cards for. This account just holds all incoming revenue for a period of time (usually around two weeks) before being "swept" into the other four accounts that you will use to run your business and your life.

The first account is the Profit account. This is where the game-changing thinking of Michalowicz comes in. We start with profit. Profit in his world is not what is left over. Profit is taken out first, or there is a high probability that it will not be taken out at all!

Remember, profit is a tool that you can leverage to fuel your calling.

We like to say, "Profit is profit." Huh? Well, if I lined up twenty business owners and asked them how they calculate profit, we would likely get twenty different responses. The calculation of profit is actually pretty straightforward; it is the money you set aside first and is not required for any payback, reinvestment, or liability.

If you prioritize profit, you will have the margin to fund your calling. If you do not, then you will constantly be chasing your tail.

Each account you establish will have a predefined percentage that you will assign to it. We will get into the details of that here in just a bit. The percentage that you will associate with this account will usually be anywhere from 1% to 20%. It all depends, but more on percentages in each account later. Bottom line, make sure you have an account set up titled Profit. This can be a savings account since you will not be writing checks or swiping a debit card from this account.

The profit that builds up in this account will serve as your "owner draw" that you will take during each quarter of the year. Michalowicz recommends the first of each quarter taking 50% of whatever is in the Profit account at that time as a draw, so you can enjoy some now and so there is always a "rainy-day fund" for you and your family.

What you draw is money set aside for whatever you want. Charitable contributions over and above your normal giving, college savings, maxing out retirement plans, vacations, jet skis, or a new chicken coop. It is totally up to you. Remember, it is the psychological "thank you" for taking the risk to start a great business.

Under no circumstance are the funds in the Profit account meant to be used for reinvestment back into the business, so adjust your percentage accordingly. Why? Your business needs to operate on a defined percentage that *includes* reinvestment, cost of goods, and capital expenditures. Without getting too deep in detail—again, get the *Profit First* book for more specifics—just make sure you have a defined percentage. Then, "flush" that percentage into your profit account from your Income account with the frequency you have preset. More on that frequency later as well.

The second account you will be setting up is the Owner's Compensation account. You as an owner need to be fairly compensated for the work that you are performing for the business. Paying everyone else except yourself is not a sustainable model. This is the difference between running a hobby and running a business. Hobbies do not compensate their owners financially; businesses do.

The Owner's Compensation account is a bucket that you are setting up to be compensated from. If you as the owner are receiving a payroll check from your business, then you can transfer funds from your owner account to the fourth account that you will be setting up called the "Operating Expense" account. One point of clarification: There is a difference between total revenue and real revenue.

For instance, if you run a business that is heavy on subcontractors and material like homebuilding is, your total revenue is *all* of the money that you receive. Your real revenue is all of the money you receive minus what you pay your subcontractors and materials. A homebuilding company may do $14 million worth of revenue in a year, but if their materials and subcontractor labor (not including office employees) are 75%, then their real revenue is . . .

$$\$14,000,000 - 75\% = \$3,500,000$$

The $3,500,000 is their real revenue. In other words, they are running a $3,500,000 company. The rest is simply passing through from the customer to the subcontractors and materials.

Contractors and companies that rely heavily on subcontractors and cost of goods sold (COGS) find themselves with these two numbers (total revenue and real revenue); everyone else will classify all of their income as real revenue.

Back to the accounts.

So far, we have the Income account where all incoming revenue is deposited.

Then, we have the Profit account where we can begin realizing profit immediately.

Next, we have set up the Owner's Compensation account. So far, all of these can be savings accounts since you will only be using them as a feature of your online banking and only need to write bank checks from them.

The third account in this base model is the Tax account. Ah yes, the tax man. As crazy as it sounds, having this account set up will actually give you great freedom knowing that this liability is taken care of. This is your "stay out of jail" account or your "sleep well at night knowing you can pay the tax man" account. The Profit First model recommends roughly 15% in this account that should cover the majority of your tax liability since you are not taxed on your legitimate business expenses. Again, please consult your financial professional for the exact percentage you should be setting aside.

You will write a direct bank check from this account to the appropriate entities for your estimated tax liabilities throughout the year.

Now back to the Operating Expense account, the fourth account. Your Operating Expense account will be a checking account that you will actually run your entire business from (Unless you have a sixth account set up for subcontractors and materials. Again, for those who have a significant portion of revenue going to those categories, we'll discuss this in a minute). All your regular nontax operating expenses; marketing, entertainment, payroll, meals, rent, insurance, and others will all come out of the Operating Expense account.

You will have checks and debit cards that are tied to this account, which is why it will need to be a checking account. This is also the account that will fluctuate the most.

There is a sixth possible account that you may want to

establish if you have business requiring a significant amount of revenue directed toward subcontractors and materials. It has a novel name; we call it the Subs & Materials account.

When revenue comes into your Income account, you can find the percentage that goes to subcontractors and materials (hopefully you can determine this through your financial reporting) and flush that percentage into this account. This may have to be a checking account also, unless you can write direct bank checks exclusively for your subcontractors and materials.

Once you have flushed that percentage to the Subs & Materials account, then you can take 100% of what is remaining and flush that to the four main accounts; Profit, Owner's Compensation, Tax, and Operating Expense.

How do you choose the percentages in each account? Let's start with what we know. The tax man is going to get his. That percentage has been set for you. Again, we follow Michalowicz's advice and set that to be 15% of our real revenue. Our CPA is the one who ultimately tells us exactly what the tax liability is, and yours should also.

Then, let's go to the Profit account. We know we want to be profitable *right now*, so let's just put 1% as the profit number for now. We can always come back and adjust.

So far, we have used up 16% of our allotted 100% that we can flush from the Income account to our four primary accounts. We have 84% remaining.

Moving to the Owner's Compensation account, how

much do you need to live on? Let's say that added up to 32% of total average income. So we put 32% in the Owner's Compensation account.

Now let's go to the Operating Expense Account. So far, with Tax at 15%, Profit at 1%, and Owner's Compensation at 32%, we have used up 48% of our 100% allotment. Now we know we can put as much as 52% into our Operation Expense account.

Before we do, think about your worst income month and your highest expense month. This is the proverbial "worst-case scenario." What percentage of operating expense would you need to run the business in the month of your highest expense? Is it less than 52%?

If so, you know you can give some of that percentage over to Profit and raise that account.

Let's say for example that you can run the business in "worst-case scenario" on 50%. Then, let's take that 2% difference and move it to the Profit account, where we will raise our profit from 1% to 3%.

You might say, "Well, I thought we ran a 10% margin?!?!" That is what you thought. That is why we are doing it this way. Remember, it is not what the spreadsheet says; it is what you can actually cash out of your bank account.

If you find these percentages to be too low or too high, feel free to adjust them monthly or quarterly in order to get to the right mix.

How often should you flush the Income account? Michalowicz recommends on the 10th and 25th of the month to create consistency and also revolve around the beginning and end of month cycles. Candidly, for us, we flush the Income account every two weeks on Sunday night. It is just easier for us that way.

To begin our initial flush, we took the amount that was in our one account, split it up by these percentages, and made the transfers, which can all be done online. You may have to play around with the cash flow on the first disbursement, and then, you can begin in two weeks do your regular flush amounts.

The *Profit First* book contains a variety of examples in percentages that different businesses use depending on their size and revenue flows.

By the way, we practice what we preach. Here is an actual snapshot of our online bank account titles. This has *changed the game* for us.

OPEX

TAX ACCOUNT

OWNERS PAY

PROFIT

INCOME

Setting this up will help you to be profitable immediately. You will begin seeing some real fruit in your bank account versus perceived fruit on a spreadsheet.

Some of you will be skeptical. I go back to the question I asked earlier about your current setup. How is it working for you? We want you to be profitable *right now* and not just on paper, and this is the most straightforward way we have seen to make that happen.

The *Profit First* book has a great tool called the "Instant Assessment" that will help you build a simple bank account road map.

Build the road map, go set up the accounts at your bank, share it with your bookkeeper and CPA, and start conquering the chaos with *real* profit.

Road Map Two:
Your Chaos-Conquering
Nonnegotiable Weekly Schedule

Making the Time

Benjamin Franklin said, "He that is good for making excuses is seldom good for anything else."

The entire leadership team of a heroic small business was on the coaching call with me when Michelle, the office manager, had enough. Michelle broke down on the coaching call and screamed out, "Everyone keeps interrupting me!"

Two weeks prior, we had worked methodically and excitedly through a weekly schedule that prioritized all of the items on her job role in appropriate blocks of time and days that the work needed to be done.

After building it out, Michelle and the rest of the team realized that she would have more marginal time than she thought to research new items for the business and also have a little breathing room to make sure everything in her role was completed according to process. Michelle had massive anticipation for how something so simple would work out and allow her to truly feel like she was "doing her job" instead of constantly submitting to chaos by putting out petty fires.

As the weeks moved along, Michelle reviewed her non-negotiable weekly schedule in the morning and by about 9:30 A.M., chaos had begun to take control, and by 10:00 A.M., Michelle was totally discouraged and back to her all-too-familiar role as a nonheroic small-business firefighter. All of the tasks seemed urgent, but few of them felt important to the mission of the business.

She knew what the problem was and in no way felt comfortable identifying it out loud or doing anything to change it. As all frustrations and truths finally do, it erupted to the surface during our coaching call—for all to hear.

"Everyone keeps interrupting me!"

Some of the most powerful tools I have in my coaching toolbelt are simple and direct questions. Michelle's unintended confession surfaced on the heels of one of my coaching questions. I asked, "What is getting in the way of you sticking to your nonnegotiable weekly schedule?"

"Everyone keeps interrupting me!"

Like any villain, chaos never presents in its own form. Instead, chaos embodies other people so that we lose our temper with them while chaos is allowed to skirt free as we stew on the person and not on the truth.

The reason everyone was interrupting Michelle is because *they* were slow dancing with chaos and wanted to stop and pass chaos on to someone else to handle it.

The typical victims of such abdication are personalities

who are passive and people-centric. These personalities typically dislike saying no, being offensive, and maneuvering through confrontation, so they are prone to "yes" their way right back into the devilish arms of chaos when a business owner or another team member offers a dance.

When anyone decides to dance with chaos they are, as John Mayer eloquently writes, "slow dancing in a burning room." It is just a matter of time before incineration.

I have gone around and around trying to find a deeply quotable way to say this, but none comes, so I will lay it out simply. If you do not implement a weekly schedule, you will dance with chaos until you dance no more.

Your time is *your* time, and you will never be able to repeat or replicate it. Unless you deeply desire a life of anxiety, depression, and never measuring up, then start living within the *restriction* of a weekly schedule and stop dancing with chaos.

That is right. Weekly schedules are intentionally *restrictive*. They set boundaries, and boundaries breed freedom. Without the boundary of sleep, I am unable to write this book, and you are unable to implement it.

The nonnegotiable weekly schedule is a clearly defined road map of how and where you spend your time built completely on each person's written job role (later in this book) and *not* on a leader's haphazard crisis du jour.

Before I show you the piece-of-cake approach to building a usable nonnegotiable weekly schedule, please promise me this, and say it out loud: when we build our nonnegotiable weekly schedules, I will live by mine and give others the freedom to live by theirs.

The great distractor of a person's weekly schedule is not the other person . . . it is you.

If someone asks you to do something now that is not in line with your schedule, do not be rude, just ask a simple question:

"I am happy to do that for you. Right now, I am spending a focused block of time (see Cal Newport and his great book *Deep Work*) working on (insert subject) right now due to my weekly schedule. Would you like for me to stop work on that and work on your request instead?"

Make that person decide if they are going to be the one putting the business at risk by not staying focused on the important while the urgent screams in the background.

If you say "yes" to their request, you are saying "no" to something else. That is okay . . . as long as it is clearly communicated.

How to Build Your Nonnegotiable Weekly Schedule Road Map

This process cannot be completed in a vacuum. You need to build this with the perspective of tools and people, because your work does not just affect you.

A couple of items that we will need to get started on building out your weekly schedule are a spreadsheet and your written job role (we will actually work through how to build a job role later in the book). A job role is a list of the big bucket items that your role will entail. If you are the bookkeeper, then your role may look something like this:

Accounts Payable

Reviewing Invoices/Bills

Reviewing Bills to Bids

Check Preparation

Accounts Receivable

Aging Reports

Client Communication/Follow-Up

Invoicing

Receiving Billings from Team

Preparing/Sending Invoices

Customer Follow-Up

Team Communication

Monthly Cash Update Meeting

Weekly Team Meeting

Your job role *must* be written. Michael Gerber said, "If you don't write it down, you don't own it." Dang straight. Stand up when you preach, Michael Gerber!

Please do not write out a weekly schedule until you have a written job role or else you are just making things up as you go, a clear sign that chaos has entered the building. The role will allow you to see the big items that need to begin populating your weekly schedule.

Spreadsheet Setup

Open a spreadsheet and put the days of the week across the top and the times of the day down the left-hand column (at least in 30-minute blocks).

A	B	C	D	E	F
	Monday	Tuesday	Wednesday	Thursday	Friday
700					
730					
800					
830					
900					
930					
1000					
1030					
1100					
1130					
1200					
1230					
100					
130					
200					
230					
300					
330					
400					
430					
500					
530					

Notable goal-setting and leader training organizations like Steven Covey and Franklin Covey planning systems talk about big rocks and small rocks. Big rocks must go into your "jar" or schedule first to ensure adequate space, followed by the smaller rocks that will begin to fill in the empty spaces. If you try to put things into your metaphorical jar in the wrong order, it will not all fit.

Once you have a spreadsheet set up, you will look at your written job role and pick the two, three, or four big rocks.

These are items that *must* be done and take a significant chunk of time. It could be team meetings, payroll, site visits, sales calls, data entry, anything that is a substantive piece of your role that would be hard to move around.

You will take those items and think through the days and times they need to be completed, and slot those first. Do not forget to look at your weekly schedule through the lens of what time of the day you are most energized and focused to do that particular task, and begin to build it from scratch.

Here is an example of placing some big rocks.

A	B Monday	C Tuesday	D Wednesday	E Thursday	F Friday	G Saturday
700	Manager Meeting	Morning Huddles	Morning Huddles	Morning Huddles	Morning Huddles	
730	Manager Meeting					
800	Manager Meeting	Weekly Ops Meeting				
830	Estimating	Weekly Ops Meeting				
900	Estimating	Weekly Ops Meeting				
930	Estimating	Estimating				
1000	Architecture Meeting	Estimating			Architecture Huddle - Leads	
1030	Architecture Meeting	Coaching	Architecture Huddle - Leads			
1100		Coaching	Email	Email	Email	
1130		Coaching	Email	Email	Email	
1200	Email	Email				
1230	Email	Email				
100						
130						
200						
230						
300						
330						
400					Prep For Next Week	
430					Prep For Next Week	
500						
530						

From the big rocks, we then go back to our written job role, pick up all of the other tasks, and place those throughout the weekly schedule, with one caveat.

You must leave at least a few hours of blank space in your week to maneuver tasks around so that when legitimate emergencies do arise, they can be handled as tasks instead of chaotic urgencies that ruin everything. Also, this blank space serves as marginal time necessary to do the deep work of being an Owner.

In the example above, if the only time a client can meet is on Tuesday at 9:30 A.M., that is no problem; all you do is move "Estimating" to one of those blank spaces and take the client meeting.

This is usually where someone will push back and ask about all of the fires that pop up during the day. Honestly, most of those fires exist because you have chosen to not live your business life within the boundaries of a nonnegotiable weekly schedule. When your schedule is set and you are living by it, you will find that the chaos-induced fires still exist, but they are well outside of your boundaries, so you can just let them smolder.

Here is an example of a schedule laid out with room for blank spaces.

A	B Monday	C Tuesday	D Wednesday	E Thursday	F Friday	G Saturday
700	Manager Meeting	Morning Huddles	Morning Huddles	Morning Huddles	Morning Huddles	Saturday
730	Manager Meeting		Admin	Admin	Admin	
800	Manager Meeting	Weekly Ops Meeting	Admin	Admin	Admin	
830	Estimating	Weekly Ops Meeting	Admin	Admin	Admin	
900	Estimating	Weekly Ops Meeting	Admin	Admin	Appointments/Job Check Up	
930	Estimating	Estimating	Appointments/Job Check Up	Appointments/Job Check Up	Appointments/Job Check Up	
1000	Architecture Meeting	Estimating	Appointments/Job Check Up	Appointments/Job Check Up	Architecture Huddle - Leads	
1030	Architecture Meeting	Coaching	Architecture Huddle - Leads	Appointments/Job Check Up	Admin	
1100		Coaching	Email	Email	Email	
1130		Coaching	Email	Email	Email	
1200	Email	Email	Service/Quality (Follow Up) Work			
1230	Email	Email	Service/Quality (Follow Up) Work			
100	Admin	Appointments/Job Check Up	Service/Quality (Follow Up) Work	Appointments/Job Check Up	Appointments/Job Check Up	
130	Admin	Appointments/Job Check Up		Appointments/Job Check Up	Appointments/Job Check Up	
200	Appointments/Job Check Up	Appointments/Job Check Up		Appointments/Job Check Up	Appointments/Job Check Up	
230	Appointments/Job Check Up	Appointments/Job Check Up	Appointments/Job Check Up	Appointments/Job Check Up	Appointments/Job Check Up	
300	Appointments/Job Check Up	Appointments/Job Check Up	Appointments/Job Check Up	Appointments/Job Check Up	Appointments/Job Check Up	
330	Appointments/Job Check Up	Appointments/Job Check Up	Appointments/Job Check Up	Appointments/Job Check Up	Appointments/Job Check Up	
400	Appointments/Job Check Up	Appointments/Job Check Up	Appointments/Job Check Up	Appointments/Job Check Up	Prep For Next Week	
430	Appointments/Job Check Up		Appointments/Job Check Up	Appointments/Job Check Up	Prep For Next Week	
500						
530						

There is one more major factor in the successful implementation of a powerful, chaos-conquering weekly schedule: communication.

You must communicate the schedule with yourself daily, with your team initially, and then again weekly. Your weekly team meeting should have a space on the agenda to review weekly team meetings that will allow everyone to see where everyone is.

We worked this simple concept with the team at Reed Group, a land-development and real estate company, and the next week when I walked in, everyone had their schedule posted on their doors. They have chosen to see chaos as an ugly dance partner and are walking in the freedom of implementing the nonnegotiable weekly schedule.

You know the drill. Set aside thirty minutes, build a simple spreadsheet, and start filling it out based on your written job role. Start with big rocks, then small rocks, and leave room for blank spaces.

From there, set a time with your team to communicate your new schedule, and let them know that if they ask you to do something that is not on your schedule, your response will be, "I am happy to do that for you. Right now, I am spending a focused block of time working on (insert subject) due to my weekly schedule. Would you like for me to stop work on that and work on your request instead?"

It is not rude; it is thoughtful because you are putting

the mission of the business in the driver's seat, and you are putting chaos in the gutter.

What if you do your weekly schedule and realize that there is legitimately not enough time in the day to complete your tasks? The next road map will empower other people to live out their narrow brilliance while you live out yours.

Road Map Three:
Chaos-Conquering Delegation
Road Map

Sharing the Tasks

"They just don't do it the same way I do it." That would technically be very correct. They do not in fact do it the same way you do it, but sometimes they do it *better,* if you stand back and let them try. There are thousands of moving parts in a business, and most are intricate and small.

Ironically, the small parts bias themselves to consuming the majority of our time. Email is small, yet we spend the *majority* of our working day staring at it and responding to it, as if chaos did not find its home in our inbox. The most telling quote I have heard about email is that "It is someone else's agenda for your day."

Yes, it is, and chaos loves knocking you onto someone else's agenda.

The small items are precisely the ones we need to automate and outsource to other people or technologies so that we can spend our creative capacity on things that will progress the business forward to our mission.

Electronic Transactions Association released a *study* in 2016 of almost 600 small-business owners and found that one hour of a small-business owner's time was worth at least $170 per hour. Informally discussing with our clients through regular coaching sessions, we have found that number to be very conservative and often going no less than $200 per hour up to $1,000 per hour depending on the margins of the business.

What does that mean?

It means that if you as the business owner are making bank runs of an hour a week and you could find someone else to perform that task for you at $13 per hour, then you are costing your business at least $157 per hour for every bank run you make (Your time valued at $170 per hour minus the employee's time of $13 per hour).

Recently I got a new iPhone. I have used Apple products since 2004, and can count on one finger the problems I have had. But with the new phone, none of my non-Apple apps would load. I visited two Apple stores, visited with two Apple technicians via chat, and spent hours trying to solve the riddle of this phone and the key apps that we use to serve to coach our heroic small-business owners and their teams.

The Apple team members have been pleasant, kind, and solution-driven, but to no avail thus far. It finally hit me that based on my role as the owner, it is costing Business

On Purpose $200 per hour for me to click all of these buttons when my time could be better spent serving. I stopped immediately.

Do not fall into that trap!

We stall our business when we spend time on things that lie outside of our narrow brilliance and when there are others who actually love dealing with these items.

Rory Vaden, author of *Procrastinate on Purpose* tempts us to delegate with a formula that he shows to bring a 733% return on your time investment, and he explains it through what he calls the "30 X's Principle."

It goes something like this:

- 5 min task X 30 = 150 minutes of training
- 150 minutes of training = Someone else doing that five-minute task X 250 working days
- 1250 minutes of working *done by someone else*

Your 150 minutes just turned into 1,250 minutes in the first year alone!

That is a 733% return on investment on one five-minute task!

If I were a shareholder in your business and I found out that you were spending your time doing data entry in your own QuickBooks, calling Apple tech support for hours, making runs to the local office supply store to get what you need, and standing in line at the DMV to get a tag for your company vehicle, I would be less than pleased knowing your time is better spent around your narrow brilliance!

Not only can other people do those things, but there are people on this earth who *love* to do those things. When you go to the office supply store as a small-business owner, not only are you spending time and money outside of your role, but you are also robbing someone else of the opportunity to do what they love.

Abby and Jessie are two of our virtual team members, and although you may have never seen them on tour, they are rock stars.

Here is a message I just sent to Jessie when something popped into my mind while I was writing this:

Jessie and Abby not only *can* do many things, they *enjoy* doing (most of) them. You may think, "Well it only takes four minutes for me to log on, search for something I want to buy, place the order, and then have it shipped. I can just do it myself." The problem is not always the actual time it takes you. It is the fact that you are jumping out of a position of what Cal Newport calls "Deep Work" to focus on something that is fragmented and will compete for your attention.

Newport defines deep work as "the act of focusing without distraction on a cognitively demanding task" and argues that it is a sort of "superpower within our economy." Conversely, "(shallow works) tends to not create much new value in the world and are easy to replicate."

Work is not the problem. Work is great. Work has the power to serve others while enjoying satisfaction from that work simultaneously. In Kevin DeYoung's book *Crazy Busy*, he explains that "the busyness that's bad is not the busyness of work but the busyness that works hard at the wrong things." When you do nonowner things, you are working hard at the wrong things *if* you can find someone else to handle those tasks for you at a lesser cost so you can spend time focused on the non-automated, more ambiguous things that will move the business forward.

Let's also not gloss over the reality of where we spend our day as Newport shows in highlighting a 2012 study published by McKinsey, which finds "the average knowledge worker now spends more than 60 percent of the workweek engaged in electronic communication and internet searching, with close to 30 percent of a worker's time dedicated to reading and answering email."

Why do we do that to ourselves? Of course, there is some level of neuronal hit that we receive when we have responded to a quick email or text falsely communicating, "Hey, you're really getting stuff done!" Seriously, when was the last time you felt genuinely accomplished in your day because you received and sent 100 emails? Sending and receiving emails can never solve the problems of families and individuals, but important work can.

How do we free ourselves then from the tyranny of the mundane and non-urgent and equip others to be able to "do it the way we would do it?" We have to sell ourselves on the reality that delegation really does work.

If delegation is the "act of entrusting a task to another person," then let us go back to one thing that must be in place before the transfer of that task can begin.

Surgeons and operating teams came to a joint conclusion, based in part on a compelling study published by the esteemed *New England Journal of Medicine* in 2009, that delegating, and quite frankly, subjecting their standing surgical knowledge to a simple checklist raises the probability of their patient living through the procedure.

In the study entitled "A Surgical Safety Checklist to Reduce Morbidity and Mortality in a Global Population," Dr. Alex B. Haynes et al penned the conclusion that "implementation of the checklist was associated with concomitant reductions in the rates of death and complications among patients at least 16 years of age who were undergoing non-cardiac surgery in a diverse group of hospitals." The rate of death prior to the checklist was 1.5% of patients. After the checklist was introduced, the rate of death was nearly cut in half at a rate of 0.8% of patients.

Delegating tasks to other people and/or technologies, while simultaneously delegating our minds to things as simple as a paper checklist, has the potential to save lives or at least make us less grumpy!

Where do we begin?

The delegation road map is a step-by-step approach to getting everything out on a sheet of paper. Clarity is attained by laying out all of the parts and pieces so you can see broadly. The delegation road map will do that. Below is the entire road map that hundreds of small-business owners have completed along with step-by-step instructions.

Regardless of delegating tasks to another human or to a technology, the idea of delegation harnesses to exponential power of others to get the right things done. Delegation is the ultimate team player. I read a story describing a Canadian ox pull. One ox was able to pull 8,000 pounds. When two oxen were yoked together, they pulled 26,000 pounds.

Chaos stands back and takes great pleasure in you doing all of the heavy lifting. Push chaos in the lake, and begin delegating.

STEP TWO: DESIGNING YOUR CHAOS-CONQUERING ROAD MAPS

I will walk you through each step first (see Steps 1–7), and then you will walk through the tool yourself to come up with a detailed list of your "narrow brilliance" and a list of things that you can delegate *right now* (Step 8).

- **Step 1**—Write down *everything* you do currently in your role.

- **Step 2**—Write down anything you *do not* currently do but would like to.

- **Step 3**—Answer two questions on every item from Step 1.
  - 1st Question—Does this give you energy?
    - UP: This activity gives me energy.
    - NEUTRAL: This activity neither gives nor consumes energy.
    - DOWN: This activity drains me of energy.
  - 2nd Question—Do you *have* to do this or can someone else do it 80% as good as you after reasonable training?
    - I *must* do this.
    - I *feel like* I need to do this.
    - I *could* delegate this to someone who could do it 80% as well as I can with reasonable training.

- **Step 4**—Make a list of anything that is marked with an "up" arrow regardless of the response to the 2nd Question.

- **Step 5**—Make a list of anything that is ranked as a 2 or 3 from Step 3 that is either neutral or drains you of energy.

- **Step 6**—Take your list of Step 5 and delegate each item by answering these questions on each.
  - Who has the capability to **own** this?
  - How will I **train** the new owner of this?
  - How will I **track**/account for progress?
  - When will I **delegate** this?

- **Step 7**—Take your list from Step 4 and build your new role out of this list. This is your "narrow brilliance." Now build your new schedule around this list. Fight the voices in your head telling you, "It is not that easy!!!"
  Who cares what *they* say! It is not *their* responsibility to live out what God has naturally put inside of you . . . it is yours alone.

- **Step 8**—IMPLEMENT AND DO IT!!

Your turn!

Step 1—Make another spreadsheet and write down *everything* you do currently in your role. . . .

Activity	Time	Energy	Rank	$	Currently delegated
Invoicing	120	neutral	3	$400.00	yes
PodWrench development	240	up	2	$800.00	no
Sponsor outreach	180	down	3	$600.00	no
Podcast Scheduling	60	down	3	$200.00	no
Sponsor upkeep	20	down	3	$66.67	yes
Setting up conference websites	60	down	3	$200.00	yes
Sponsor outreach	60	neutral	3	$200.00	no
Podcast Scheduling	60	neutral	3	$200.00	no
Sponsor upkeep	10	neutral	3	$33.33	no
Setting up conference websites	60	down	3	$200.00	yes
Sponsor outreach	20	neutral	3	$66.67	no
Podcast Scheduling	60	neutral	2	$200.00	no
Sponsor upkeep	60	neutral	3	$200.00	no
Promoting podcast episodes	60	down	3	$200.00	no
Recording podcasts	240	up	1	$800.00	yes
Finding new podcast hosts	10	down	2	$33.33	yes
Preparing slides for courses	180	down	2	$600.00	no
Recording courses	90	up	1	$300.00	no
Scheduling other calls and events	30	down	3	$100.00	

Step 2—In the same column, write down anything you *do not* currently do, but would like to. . . .

Activity	Time	Energy	Rank	$	Currently delegated
Invoicing	120	neutral	3	$400.00	yes
PodWrench development	240	up	2	$800.00	no
Sponsor outreach	180	down	3	$600.00	no
Podcast Scheduling	60	down	3	$200.00	no
Sponsor upkeep	20	down	3	$66.67	yes
Setting up conference websites	60	down	3	$200.00	yes
Sponsor outreach	60	neutral	3	$200.00	no
Podcast Scheduling	60	neutral	3	$200.00	no
Sponsor upkeep	10	neutral	3	$33.33	no
Setting up conference websites	60	down	3	$200.00	yes
Sponsor outreach	20	neutral	3	$66.67	no
Podcast Scheduling	60	neutral	2	$200.00	no
Sponsor upkeep	60	neutral	3	$200.00	no
Promoting podcast episodes	60	down	3	$200.00	no
Recording podcasts	240	up	1	$800.00	yes
Finding new podcast hosts	10	down	2	$33.33	yes
Preparing slides for courses	180	down	2	$600.00	no
Recording courses	90	up	1	$300.00	no

Step 3—Go back to your list from Step 1 and answer the four questions on every item (arrows and numbers).

How much time does it take in minutes per week?

Activity	Time	Energy	Rank	$	Currently delegated
Invoicing	120	neutral	3	$400.00	yes
PodWrench development	240	up	2	$800.00	no
Sponsor outreach	180	down	3	$600.00	no
Podcast Scheduling	60	down	3	$200.00	no
Sponsor upkeep	20	down	3	$66.67	yes
Setting up conference websites	60	down	3	$200.00	yes
Sponsor outreach	60	neutral	3	$200.00	no
Podcast Scheduling	60	neutral	3	$200.00	no
Sponsor upkeep	10	neutral	3	$33.33	no
Setting up conference websites	60	down	3	$200.00	yes
Sponsor outreach	20	neutral	3	$66.67	no
Podcast Scheduling	60	neutral	2	$200.00	no
Sponsor upkeep	60	neutral	3	$200.00	no
Promoting podcast episodes	60	down	3	$200.00	no
Recording podcasts	240	up	1	$800.00	yes
Finding new podcast hosts	10	down	2	$33.33	yes
Preparing slides for courses	180	down	2	$600.00	no
Recording courses	90	up	1	$300.00	no

Does this give energy (up), take away energy (down), or leave you at the same level (neutral)?

Activity	Time	Energy	Rank	$	Currently delegated
Invoicing	120	neutral	3	$400.00	yes
PodWrench development	240	up	2	$800.00	no
Sponsor outreach	180	down	3	$600.00	no
Podcast Scheduling	60	down	3	$200.00	no
Sponsor upkeep	20	down	3	$66.67	yes
Setting up conference websites	60	down	3	$200.00	yes
Sponsor outreach	60	neutral	3	$200.00	no
Podcast Scheduling	60	neutral	3	$200.00	no
Sponsor upkeep	10	neutral	3	$33.33	no
Setting up conference websites	60	down	3	$200.00	yes
Sponsor outreach	20	neutral	3	$66.67	no
Podcast Scheduling	60	neutral	2	$200.00	no
Sponsor upkeep	60	neutral	3	$200.00	no
Promoting podcast episodes	60	down	3	$200.00	no
Recording podcasts	240	up	1	$800.00	yes
Finding new podcast hosts	10	down	2	$33.33	yes
Preparing slides for courses	180	down	2	$600.00	no
Recording courses	90	up	1	$300.00	no

Is this (a) something *only* you can do, (b) something you *thought* only you could do, or (c) something that should have been delegated long ago??

Activity	Time	Energy	Rank	$	Currently delegated
Invoicing	120	neutral	3	$400.00	yes
PodWrench development	240	up	2	$800.00	no
Sponsor outreach	180	down	3	$600.00	no
Podcast Scheduling	60	down	3	$200.00	no
Sponsor upkeep	20	down	3	$66.67	yes
Setting up conference websites	60	down	3	$200.00	yes
Sponsor outreach	60	neutral	3	$200.00	no
Podcast Scheduling	60	neutral	3	$200.00	no
Sponsor upkeep	10	neutral	3	$33.33	no
Setting up conference websites	60	down	3	$200.00	yes
Sponsor outreach	20	neutral	3	$66.67	no
Podcast Scheduling	60	neutral	2	$200.00	no
Sponsor upkeep	60	neutral	3	$200.00	no
Promoting podcast episodes	60	down	3	$200.00	no
Recording podcasts	240	up	1	$800.00	yes
Finding new podcast hosts	10	down	2	$33.33	yes
Preparing slides for courses	180	down	2	$600.00	no
Recording courses	90	up	1	$300.00	no

If the average billable rate of a business owner is a *mini-mum* of $200 per hour, how much money is this task costing your business?

Activity	Time	Energy	Rank	$	Currently delegated
Invoicing	120	neutral	3	$400.00	yes
PodWrench development	240	up	2	$800.00	no
Sponsor outreach	180	down	3	$600.00	no
Podcast Scheduling	60	down	3	$200.00	no
Sponsor upkeep	20	down	3	$66.67	yes
Setting up conference websites	60	down	3	$200.00	yes
Sponsor outreach	60	neutral	3	$200.00	no
Podcast Scheduling	60	neutral	3	$200.00	no
Sponsor upkeep	10	neutral	3	$33.33	no
Setting up conference websites	60	down	3	$200.00	yes
Sponsor outreach	20	neutral	3	$66.67	no
Podcast Scheduling	60	neutral	2	$200.00	no
Sponsor upkeep	60	neutral	3	$200.00	no
Promoting podcast episodes	60	down	3	$200.00	no
Recording podcasts	240	up	1	$800.00	yes
Finding new podcast hosts	10	down	2	$33.33	yes
Preparing slides for courses	180	down	2	$600.00	no
Recording courses	90	up	1	$300.00	no

Step 4—Make a list of anything that is marked with an "up" arrow regardless of the response to the "2nd Question."

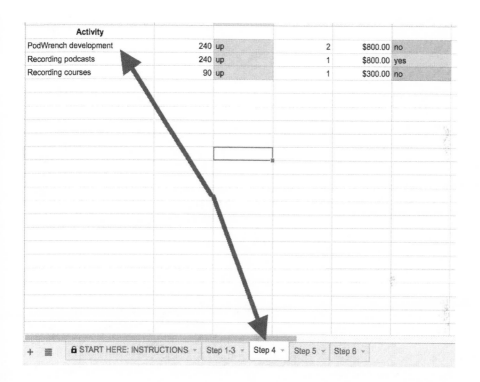

Step 5—Make a list of anything that is ranked as a #2 or #3 and is either neutral or drains you of energy.

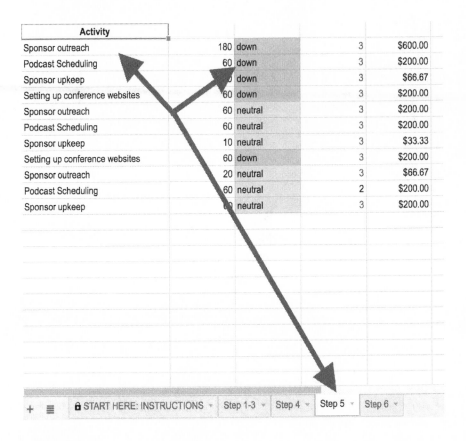

Activity				
Sponsor outreach	180	down	3	$600.00
Podcast Scheduling	60	down	3	$200.00
Sponsor upkeep		down	3	$66.67
Setting up conference websites	60	down	3	$200.00
Sponsor outreach	60	neutral	3	$200.00
Podcast Scheduling	60	neutral	3	$200.00
Sponsor upkeep	10	neutral	3	$33.33
Setting up conference websites	60	down	3	$200.00
Sponsor outreach	20	neutral	3	$66.67
Podcast Scheduling	60	neutral	2	$200.00
Sponsor upkeep		neutral	3	$200.00

+ ≡ 🔒 START HERE: INSTRUCTIONS ▾ | Step 1-3 ▾ | Step 4 ▾ | Step 5 ▾ | Step 6 ▾

Step 6—Take your list from Step 5, and delegate each possible item by answering these questions on each.

Who has the capability to own this?

How will I train the new owner of this?

How will I track/account for progress?

When will I delegate this?

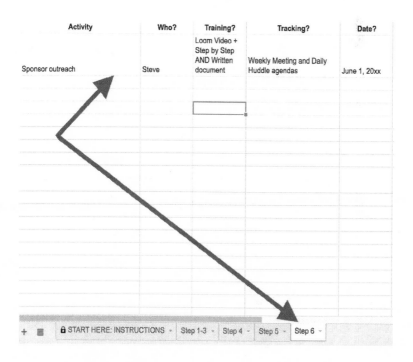

Activity	Who?	Training?	Tracking?	Date?
Sponsor outreach	Steve	Loom Video + Step by Step AND Written document	Weekly Meeting and Daily Huddle agendas	June 1, 20xx

START HERE: INSTRUCTIONS · | Step 1-3 · | Step 4 · | Step 5 · | Step 6 ·

Step 7—Take your list from Step 4 and build your new role out of this list. This is your "narrow brilliance." You may need to add anything that **absolutely could not be delegated**.

Taking this road map, you can then go back and compare it to your nonnegotiable weekly schedule and potentially free up even more time for drilling down on deep work.

I recommend that you print this list out, and keep it in a binder with you and begin writing on it every time you think about a task that you do that can be outsourced. Once you begin looking for delegable tasks, you will realize they are everywhere. That hardest part to implementation is the bonus step: doing it.

Go ahead and set aside about 60 minutes right now on your calendar. Go ahead. Do it now.

Then take that time (heads up, you will be bombarded with distractions), shut off all of the pings and dings, get to work delegating, and watch chaos pout in the corner.

Road Map Four:
Chaos-Conquering Systems
Road Map

Finding the Systems

After graduating seminary (I know, I do not really seem like the seminary type, huh?) with my Master of Divinity, I went to work for a few years at Pfizer, a global pharmaceutical company, making for an odd blueprint into the corporate world, but it all connects in the end.

Upon entering the sales force of a pharmaceutical giant, I walked into a well-oiled machine of training and preparation that made college look like kindergarten. To my best recollection, I spent one week in home study with books that were the size of a dumpster and would plow through those morning to night with earmarks, tabs, highlights, notes, and a lot of question marks. Many people know exactly where they were when the 9/11 attacks occurred. I was at my in-laws' house studying while Ashley and our daughter were in the living room witnessing the breaking news.

After passing the initial test for home study, we then went to a regional office for two weeks straight to study, take tests, and role play until we wanted to personally slash the tires of every sales trainer that we had (unless they would sneak us an answer or two).

Not done yet.

Directly after that, I spent two more weeks in New York at the Pfizer training facility that served as one part summer camp for sales reps and another part torture cell as we continued what we had started in the regional office.

Then, it was off to our home territory where we would visit local physician clinics with our district manager and try to live up to the training and the hype that we had portrayed through our hiring phase and initial training phase. It was intense and was honestly some of the best training I have ever received. It was not *fun*, but it was *good*—world-class good.

During that time, I learned more about the human body and about medical terminology than I ever knew God had invented. Study escalated my appreciation for what physicians, nurses, therapists, and other medical personnel endure to bring value and compassion to patients.

One thing I learned through all of that study (beyond how little sleep and how much anxiety I could actually function on) was that the human body is composed of eleven primary systems (cardiovascular, endocrine, skeletal, etc.). I began to see that one body is made up of eleven parts, which are each in and of themselves made up of tens, hundreds, thousands, and billions of micro parts.

For physicians to make a diagnosis so it is not so overwhelming, they will identify (even if only subconsciously) the primary system that may be home to the sign or symptom the patient is complaining about. If they are able to isolate the system, they can drill down and begin to understand the unique quirk within the larger system to be treated.

It made complete sense and seemed to be a very efficient way to target what could be thousands or millions of potential problems into categories. We humans love to categorize because it helps to simplify.

In the summer of 2018, we had the opportunity to walk through the Leonardo Da Vinci museum. Instead of being a location that housed the massive collection of unfinished paintings Da Vinci was renowned for, this was a museum where technicians went back to Da Vinci's drawings and built to scale everything that Da Vinci had drawn out in his lifetime like a hand-crank crane, a hall of mirrors, and a portable bridge structure.

Da Vinci was a man who, through his notebooks, invented technologies before they were formally "invented." He was a genius. In their quest of bringing realism to art, Da Vinci and Michelangelo were both known to dissect human cadavers to understand their underlying anatomy.

Five hundred years ago, systems played out in Da Vinci's sketches and notes.

All of this leads to a proud moment for me when I was

sitting in the conference of a hospital working with the management team through the Four Steps to Business Freedom, and we launched into building their Systems Road Map. As I was explaining it through my usual approach with metaphors, I quietly asked the team in the room (most of which were physicians or medical personnel), "How many systems make up the human body?"

I understand it is not a question they think about all day, even though it is a metaphor that I use all of the time, but I was the only one who knew the answer, leaving the entire room chuckling at the irony. Trust me, though, you still want them and not me treating you. I chalked it up to catching them off guard.

When we categorize complex things, it helps to calm our mind to see that a mountain can be climbed. This is the underlying premise in climbing a mountain (one segment at a time), treating a patient (rule out one system at a time), or eating an elephant (one bite at a time), which I still have yet to do.

If you have not read Michael Gerber's *E-Myth*, finish this book, then go read his delightfully revealing allegory about Sarah and her pie shop. If you are a small-business owner, *E-Myth* is Small Biz 101. When I read *E-Myth Revisited* more than ten years ago, I devoured it and finished it thinking, that is it! Gerber sees what so many small-business owners cannot. If I could summarize a fundamental premise in the book, it is the idea that small-business owners spend the majority of their time working in their business and not enough time or intentionality working *on* their business. As mentioned earlier, working *in* your business means *you* are producing the widget, running the invoices, following up with customers, and overwhelmed by tasks. Working *on* your business means you are spending the majority of your time training and developing *others* to produce the widgets, run the invoices, and follow up with customers so you are not overwhelmed with tasks.

Gerber's story about Sarah and her pie shop sheds light on the desperation that small-business owners have to categorize the big chunks of their business into systems and begin spending some of their time training others on how to run the system so the business owners do not have to show up every morning at 3 a.m. to start baking pies!

Right now, statistically, you are baking your own pies, doing your own books, taking out your own trash, and running around with your hair on fire saying there are so many things to do and so many things that seem undone. You are right. There *are* so many things to do and so many things that seem undone precisely because your hair *is* on fire, and you have not stopped long enough to build an extinguisher system. Until now you may not have even known that there were different systems that make up the anatomy of your business.

LET YOUR BUSINESS BURN

This is one of the most exciting parts of the process in the Four Steps to Business Freedom. We pause and for the first time put on the surgical gloves, cut the business open (gross, I know), and diagnose exactly what systems exist in your business. Remember this, where there is no vision, people scatter, and what gets you to the vision is the continual and repetitive implementation of the systems in your business.

Chaos is a cancer that at times requires medical intervention.

Sam Carpenter in his book *Work The System* talks about his revolution of business (and frankly of life) when he looked outside one day, after living in business hell for fifteen years, and realized that the world he saw was nothing more than a collection of systems working in repetition over and over again. The sun comes up and goes down every day. We live where the tide comes in and the tide comes out every six and a half hours or so. The rains come and the rains go.

All of life is a collection of systems, and the faster you as a small-business owner submit yourself to that reality, the faster you will free yourself from the chaos of working *in* your business.

How do we conduct exploratory surgery on the business, and what will we find?

Typically, when we stop and look inside the reality of your small business, we are going to find a collection of anywhere from three to six (rarely more or fewer) major systems that make up the body of your small business. For instance, many businesses have an operations system, administration system, marketing and sales system. Others I have seen have a production system, human resources system, or a safety system (usually in construction or manufacturing).

When we build a systems map, we begin noticing each system uniquely along with their component parts. For instance, your administration system may be made up of components like accounting, office supplies, licenses and fees, contracts, etc.

If you wanted to drill down further, you could find that the accounting component is made up of payables, receivables, invoicing, expense reporting, taxes, etc.

Once you begin to get all of these component parts categorized within the larger bucket of a system, you can make real progress on getting the processes within each system defined, either onto your plate at an appropriate time or onto the plate of someone else who can offer their skill set within the context of your business, that will push you toward the ultimate vision that you have already spelled out!

Ready to get your business on the surgical table and proceed with the exploratory surgery? Before we start cutting, let's first identify a few common business systems that you *could* find when you get into the body of the business.

Operations

Customer Service

Finance/Accounting

Sales

Marketing

Human Resources

Communication

Legal

Administration

Information Technology

Obviously, these are some systems that we have seen before, but you will not know what *really* exists until we get in there and have a look for ourselves. The first thing you need to do is identify other things that you think may classify as a big system within your business that is not included above. Write them out in the open space next to the list, or you can use the template that we provide in the back of this book and also at **MyBusinessOnPurpose.com/tools** and add them in the "Additional Systems" column.

Once you have written down everything in your head that you think could be a system, pick one that you know, beyond a shadow of a doubt, that describes in part a system that makes up your business. This first one is usually something pretty easy like "Administration." I have not met a business yet that does not have something to administrate behind the scenes. Feel free to call it whatever you like. This is a system in *your* business, not mine.

As a side note, the four business systems that currently make up our Business On Purpose platform are 1) Administration, 2) Marketing 3) Coaching, and 4) People.

The more systems you have, the more fragmented your business management is going to have to be down the road, so look to consolidate where possible. If you are a business of greater than $5 million annually, you will likely need four or five major systems.

Do not close up the body of your business just yet. There is one more beneficial procedure that we can do while the business is opened up to make sure that the cancer of chaos does not find a home inside.

In my work with Pfizer and in our periodic involvement in healthcare in Nigeria, I have been invited and allowed to observe many surgical cases in the operating rooms of hospitals. I am never at a loss for amazement and wonder when I watch a skilled surgeon maneuver the human body with precision, compassion, and thought. With all of the surgeries I have observed, I cannot recall a time when everything went just as planned for the surgical team. When you open up the body, you can see things with the human eye that can be elusive to the world's greatest technologies.

While your business is exposed right now, let's take a minute to diagnose the overall health of your business. Let's also take a minute to determine where we should begin with treating any disease that exist while also taking advantage of any opportunities.

On a document or a sheet of paper write "Rank Current Health" and "Priority Moving Forward," each with its own column. We want to ask a series of questions of our business based on the newly articulated systems that you have identified in your business that will allow us to *rank the current health* while determining which system should capture our focus of *priority moving forward.*

Let's use an example list of systems for this next section:

Production
Administration
Marketing
Sales

Final systems list	Rank current health	Priority moving forward
Production		
Administration		
Marketing		
Sales		

The first question to ask is "Which of the three systems that make up my business would I, hands down, without question, say is the *best* functioning of the three?" Put a number one in the "Rank Current Health" column next to that system.

The second question to ask is, which of the remaining two systems (again, using our example) is by far, without question, the *worst* functioning? Put a number three next to that system, and then since there are only three in the example, place a number two next to the remaining system. It may look like this:

Final systems list	Rank current health	Priority moving forward
Production	1	
Administration	3	
Marketing	2	
Sales	4	

This provides a simple and honest diagnosis of the current health of your business so you can see where you stand. Just because Administration is number three, though, does not necessarily mean it is the priority moving forward that leads us to our next set of questions.

While there are loads of great options and opportunity constant requesting and making demands of our time, it does not mean that every opportunity is a good one.

I do not know who the quote originated from, but my friend and co-founder of Interview Valet, Tom Schwab, made a comment to me that has stuck like a squashed mosquito on the corner of my windshield. He said, "Be aware of profitable distractions."

Ouch!

In 2016, our local area was rocked by Hurricane Matthew, a category two hurricane, whose eye was spotted less than two miles off the coast of Hilton Head Island, SC. When we were all finally allowed back in town from a mandatory evacuation, the damage was overwhelming. Ours is a geography loaded with trees, and many of our trees had been completely uprooted from the ground like stationary toothpicks. What took tens and hundreds of years to grow and build was partially dismantled in a matter of hours. It was awe-inducing and powerful.

As business began to open locally, we all took notice of the new businesses and new services that were being offered in the wake of a great tragedy. Some of the services were necessary and extraordinarily helpful to our local community. Others were invasive and disruptive. As a business coach to many local businesses, I had the privilege of fielding calls from the small-business heroes who were confused about whether or not to extend new services to help homeowners who needed repair.

For the next two weeks, many of my clients were

overwhelmed by profitable distraction after profitable distraction. Could they have made money and served the community? Yes. Would it have been a distraction from their vision, mission, and core values? Yes. They were able to answer those questions because they had taken the time to articulate their systems.

The same applies as you think through the systems that you should focus your time on in prioritization. Contrary to your own belief, you cannot do it all, that is why your hair is on fire and chaos is the gel holding it up.

Here are the next set of questions I want you to ask. As you look back at the three systems (using our example above) you have articulated, out ask these questions:

Which of the three systems, if we paid it just a *little* bit of attention, just a *little* bit of effort, would yield us *huge* results (this is the lowest hanging fruit)? Place a number one next to that system regardless of what the other number is.

Which of the remaining two systems, if we paid it *tons* of attention, with *tons* of effort, would barely the move the needle? Place a number three next to that system regardless of what the other number is.

Place your remaining numbers according to the answer to these questions.

Final systems list	Rank current health	Priority moving forward
Production	1	1
Administration	3	4
Marketing	2	3
Sales	4	2

Congratulations. For the first time, you are now able to see with your own eyes exactly the systems that make up the body of your business. You can begin categorizing, processing, training, and *delegating*. You have also completed a simple diagnostic of your business, so you now know where you need to focus your time and process building (later in the book).

Chaos has now been exposed, and you have the surgical instruments to remove it. Now, if only we could identify the team that will help you in the operating room.

Welcome to the good old-fashioned Organizational Road Map.

Road Map Five: Chaos-Conquering Organizational Road Map

Building the Team

The meat was piled on each massive piece of handmade focaccia bread. The mozzarella was fresh and doing its part to create an unrivaled decor of ingestible art. Two friends opened the Gastronomium in Florence, Italy just a couple of months prior to our visit . . . ahem, visits. The pizza was abundantly decorated with non-processed basil, tomatoes, pesto, and sundried tomatoes. You just told them size you wanted, they cut it, put it in the oven, and voila!

The ingredients these friends used on the pizza individually would have been fine. When properly and thoughtfully combined, the experience was a concert in your mouth creating a desire for a curtain call.

The Gastronomium taught me two things. First, individual ingredients explode when put together and combined thoughtfully. Second, as long as you have systems in place, your business and the roles within your business can be as unique as you would like them to be. The Gastronomium had what Marcus Lemonis calls the Three P's: people, product, and process.

The old-fashioned Org Chart or what we have lovingly referred to as the Organizational Road Map is an intentionally minimalistic document with intentional systems (taken from your Systems Road Map above) and thoughtful role titles mixed to create an overly simplistic overview of your entire business that allows the newest member of your team to have mastery of "how things are structured around here."

Think back to your first day at your first job. You walked into the organization and probably thought, "I'm sure there is a structure here. I wonder what it is." With the Organizational Road Map, you will be offering an incredible gift to every new and existing team member by giving them a quick overview of what roles exist in the business and who is responsible for what.

The Organizational Road Map is a document easily shared during the interview process, the onboarding process, the growth scaling process, the promotional process, and everything in between. This road map is meant to be shared and reviewed often, not relegated to another binder on a shelf or a corkboard in the break room and donned with a motivational quote.

When you are thinking about roles, here are some principles to hold yourself to and share with your team.

Full-Time Roles

Each role is not necessarily full-time. Just because you have a role that says "bookkeeping," it does not mean it is a full-time role. It may take eight hours a week. If you do not know how long it takes, then ask.

The next time the accounts payable processes are being completed within a workweek, time them. Add up the time, and that will determine how much is needed for bookkeeping. Rinse and repeat for every single role within the business. This will tell you who and how much time is needed for each role.

If you are going to set a 40-hour workweek, then you need to dole out 40 hours of roles to a person with time built in for team meetings and ongoing training for those roles.

Do not be afraid to admit, "This is only an eight-hour-per-week role, so let's go find someone who can work this role eight hours per week." In our new economy *34%* of American workers are performing some type of freelance work. A *Labor* Force survey shows that 40% of those freelancing are categorized as being "associate professionals." In other words, they are people waiting to be presented and trained with opportunities to serve and work the systems within your business!

There is scalable value in bringing on Virtual Assistant or Freelancing team members as a regular part of your workflow.

In many cases, a full-time employee will spend a portion of their day doing what they love to do based on skill, training, and passion. In order to round out the magically 40 hours, they will often assume tasks that do not fit their skillset but need to be completed.

As a Virtual Assistant or Freelancer, that same person can spend their entire day doing what they are passionate and skilled for in the allotted amount of time needed for those tasks, and then move on to another small business who is in need of that skillset to fill out additional time during the week.

They can spend their day giving you their best rather than giving you some of their best laced with leftovers. We have worked with Virtual Team Members for the Business On Purpose platform, since early on in our business, for things like client meetings, notes, email filtering, web development, accounting, scheduling, podcast and video editing uploading, etc.

The biggest challenge for most small-business owners lies not in knowing what needs to be done but rather in taking the plunge in the pleasant waters of Virtual Team Members and training them well with a role first mindset.

Commit now to stop being so chaotic in how roles and tasks are doled out to the people (or yourself) in your small business. Take control and begin looking at your small business as a collection of systems.

One Person, Multiple Roles

In the early days you are the owner, CEO, sales manager, operations manager, and administration manager. You also have an accounting role, marketing role, and everything in between. As time progresses and the business begins to naturally progress toward the Vision Story that you have laid out from the beginning, you will start to align the roles within the Personnel section of your Vision Story with the realities on the ground. Your business will become less haphazard and chaotic and will truly be a Business On Purpose that allows you a freedom that you have not experienced.

The Organizational Road Map is easy to build, quick to read, and leaves chaos rolling its eyes in frustration. Following are some of the major roles within every Organizational Road Map.

Owner's Role

The Owner of the business (aka "You") is responsible for the general health of the overall business. You (and your partner(s) if you have any) fly 60,000 feet above the business and notice large scale macro movements that the team on the ground may never see without that perspective.

The Owner does *not* concern herself with the weeds and thorns of the business. The Owner does not care what marketing channels are used to achieve maximum market exposure. The Owner is only interested in ensuring that the business is on track toward the Vision. The Owner is *not* the pilot of the ship. The Owner *owns* the ship and evaluates the performance of the ship from a distance to ensure one thing is achieved . . . the ultimate destination (see vision story). It is the Owner's responsibility to not only schedule the time to take these high range flights over the business regularly but also to communicate regularly, predictably, and simplistically with the day-to-day overseer (see CEO Role below).

The Black Line

We intentionally place a thick line between the Owner and the CEO even though in most small businesses they are the same human being. The black line may represent what is typically the biggest challenge of the entrepreneur and forces the E-Myth question, "are you working *in* the business, or are you working *on* the business?"

Owners work on the business, and everybody else is biased to work *in* the business with the constant challenge of delegating tasks to others. There are times that team members *under the black line* work *on* the business and are focused on strategy building, planning, outsourcing, implementing technologies, etc.

CEO Role

I participated in a training call with my friend Jaime Jay at Bottlneck.online, where we trained small-business owners on how to work well with their Virtual Assistants. As we were describing the difference between the Owner and the CEO, one of the owners responded, "I think they are the same thing." I am not an overly direct person but, ummm, NO!

Owners are different than CEOs even though they may share the same human body. Where the Owner takes periodic flights at 60,000 feet above the business looking at macro trends and climates, the CEO *hovers* five feet above the business, just enough to float around quickly while able to see details that need to be completed. The CEO cares more about detail level items than the Owner(s) yet is not crawling on the ground in the weeds to spend mental energy on issues like what kind of cracker snacks do we need to get that both yield quality and value as a perk to visiting clients. *Those are important issues* delegated to others.

The CEO ensures that the right people are on mission in the right place, at the right time, on the right project, for the right purpose, and with the right processes held by predictable and motivating accountability driving the business to the ultimate vision. The CEO ensures that the roles are articulated so that the right people are being actively recruited, researched, profiled, onboarded, and trained.

CEO Tom Crosby led Pal's Sudden Service, a small regional fast food company, to become the *only* food service business in the history of the United States to win the coveted and elusive Malcolm Baldrige National Quality *Award* designated by the United State Department of Commerce. He is so intense on training that he was asked, "What if you spend all of this time and money on training and (your employees) leave?" Crosby's powerful response revealed his leadership maturity, "What if we *don't* and they *stay?*" The CEO does not do the work; the CEO casts vision, motivates, and leads the right people to do the right work.

Systems Managers

There is no shortage of television sitcoms highlighting the plight and rhythm of life in middle management. Management is just that . . . management. The word "manage" is based in the Latin word *manus* and implies the part of the human anatomy we know as the hand. Implied also is the idea of "power over another person." However you break it down, managers and/or leaders are responsible for coordinating all resources within their scope of the organization and ensuring that those resources work and operate in a congruent flow toward the ultimate vision.

A systems manager (or leader, or whatever your title may be for these roles) reports directly to the CEO on behalf of his particular system within the business. Just because the Administration manager may have responsibility for the oversight of accounts payable or office management, it does not mean he is actually performing those functions. He may hire and train someone else or an outsider vendor to perform those processes on behalf of his system and put a process of training and accountability in place for that person. Ultimately, regardless of who is working within the system, the systems manager is the single point of accountability within his system. Something goes wrong with a component part of the system, it is the systems manager who answers for it (with accountability to the CEO) and corrects it with mission, values, and process through training.

Systems Roles

Just below the systems manager are the roles that make up the necessary parts of the system itself. Each of these are role titles and *not the names of people.* This is a massively important point. We build the business out using this principle, "Role First, People Agnostic." Of course, this does not mean that we do not care about people. In fact, just the opposite. We care *so much* for people that we want to ensure that before we make any people decisions, the role itself is completely clear.

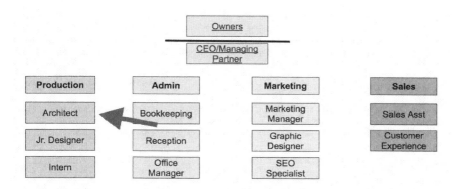

We have found that many people are disengaged in their jobs *not* because they do not like their job *but* because they are not clear on what their job is! As of this writing, *Gallup* reports that 70% of American workers are not engaged in their work. I would argue that the primary reason is because they do not have clarity as to what they are supposed to be doing or because their tasks are not properly aligned with skillset or passion.

Drawing out each individual role within the system without thinking about the particular person who plays that role sets you up perfectly to listen to what your vision story is telling you the business needs. Remember who *hates* your vision story. Chaos.

If you listen to the vision story by working through the process of building out these roles, the business will begin to bring into the picture who needs to be a part of the team and who does not. It is as if the business speaks to you rather than chaos making random and destructive suggestions.

The four elements above are couched in some larger principles as it relates to the organizational chart overall.

One caveat, and yes, I am serious . . . when you implement and this process begins to work, you are likely going to be confronted with something you now know not of: **free time.**

Beware.

Free time is a double-edged sword. You can either use it for good, or it can be gobbled up in nonsense and a newly dressed chaos (think about mid-life crisis guy). As of 2018, approximately 60–70% of Americans are scrolling around on Facebook. When you have free time in your small business, you can either use it to scroll Facebook because that is easy, *or* you can use that time for what matters most with your family or with your business. That is what your vision story is for. When growth ushers you into new business landscapes and you do not know what to do, go back to your vision story and let it speak into your next steps.

Go ahead and decide now how you are going to backfill your free time. It is time that you have purchased with hard work, diligence, training, and a whole lot of *implementation*!

Now that you have the foundation laid for the organizational chart, let's round the corner and build a game-changing that has the potential of jamming a dagger in the heart of chaos and will put your business at a level where only a few ever go.

Road Map Six:
Chaos-Conquering
Master Process Road Map

A Sellable Business

Imagine the day a lady named Josephine comes walking in your workspace, opens up a combo-locked suitcase, and says, "I am ready to buy your business at a four times multiple of your annual earnings *in cash* right here on the spot with two conditions. First, we have to be able to run your business the same *exact* way that you run your business right now, from the sales calls, to the payroll schedule, to the lead generation, to the production, and everything in between. I will not require you stay on an earn-out, but we need the entire business map so your valued customers will never feel the switch. Second, you have 30 minutes to make your decision, and we will expect the road map to be in our hands and training to begin immediately using only that road map as our training. You will not be allowed to wing any of it from your head!"

Would you do it?

You might say, "No one would ever do what Josephine did." Ummm, we have seen crazier.

Then you will say, "It is totally unreasonable to expect that a business owner would have her entire business mapped out in such detail."

Or is it?

We can say with definition that your business is certainly more "sellable" with a comprehensive road map in place, in the same way that we can say that your vacation will be infinitely more enjoyable with a road map showing you how to get there!

This entire example may be totally lost you on because you would never have the intention of selling your business anyway.

No problem.

But wouldn't you like your business to depend less on you and instead compensate you with intentional time, meaningful freedom, and the money to pay for it all?

Don't you want your business to help facilitate your passions and convictions? To serve others without killing yourself? To take chaos behind the woodshed and where you can only hear its whimpering but rarely if ever feels its impact?

We have determined through our own experience that about eight out of ten small-business owners are being *owned* by their business which means that even if they wanted to sell, they cannot. No one would ever pay to own *a business that owns them.*

How do we break out of the prison of our own business?

How do we finally get off the treadmill?

How do we stop constantly putting out fires and feeling pulled in seventeen different directions?

How do we stop the habit of throwing business Hail Marys every day?

One way to try is to continue doing things the way you have been doing them. Of course, we know where that leads-insanity and irrelevance.

The other option is to replicate the delivery of every part of our small business and make it so predictable others can run it the exact same way that we would.

Remember the old Jewish phrase?

It is God talking to the Jewish Prophet Habakkuk when he says, "Write the vision down so that those who read it may run!"

The same is true for the processes that make up the vision. In fact, we may even make our own statement to say write the *processes* down so that those who read *and implement them,* may run . . . the business.

Did you know that your business doesn't have to own you?

You do *not* have to feel like you are on a treadmill. Owning a small business does not have to feel like a daily cliff dive with no visibility and no parachute.

Owning a small business can be the ultimate opportunity to simultaneously serve customers, employees, virtual assistants, contractors, vendors, your local community, and your global community.

Business and industry were not bestowed on this earth as a curse but as a gift. Music, architecture, agriculture, and construction are given to us as gifts for us to invest time and energy in for the service of each other. We are a global network of human beings and work is a platform of mutual service to each other.

Your small business can be a massive force for living out your convictions and serving others, but it will never get there by doing the things that got you to do this point.

As I am writing this, over my screen is an incredible view of the tidal creek behind our house in the Lowcountry of South Carolina. It is a constant reminder of a real, living, breathing process created by God that just runs every day.

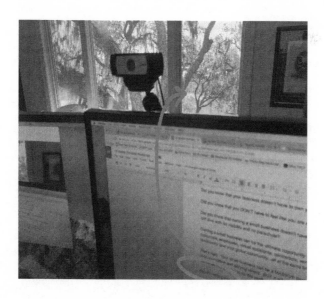

The tide comes in anywhere between seven to nine feet, and then six hours later, the creek bed is completely empty. That is right, seven to nine feet of water floods the marsh and then completely empties out every 6.5 hours. The tide comes in and the tide comes out every day!

The tides follow a process just like the earth's rotation and the seasons. Processes are simply "a series of repeatable actions or steps taken in order to achieve a particular end."

When process is not in place, what you may get is creative, but it will not be repeatable creativity. It will require new creativity *every* time. When process is in place, you experience a replication of the original creativity. I am so glad the sunset is a process, because it is something that we like to enjoy on repeat!

When you are starting your business every time you bake that cake, repair that brake, or stack that crate, you accomplish something that can be documented and processed so you never *have* to do it again.

When you process all of the individual steps, you equip and empower others to bake that cake, fix that brake, or stack that crate that allows you to focus on the other elements of serving customers like payables, receivables, inventory, and office management.

Once *those* are processed, you continue to equip and empower others to facilitate payables, receivables, inventory, and office management so you can focus on generating new leads and onboarding new customers.

Then once *those* are processed you are again equipping and empowering others to facilitate to . . .

(Hint: Rinse and Repeat.)

Do you see where this is going?

Imagine you had *every* process in your business documented, written down, and recorded with video. Heck, you could hire a full Broadway dance company to come and "perform" your processes every day. That may get a bit pricey, but, *dang*, it would be cool!

Imagine, just as NASA has *every* single detail of flying a spaceship documented, you too can have every process in your business documented.

Then, once documented, you focus the majority of your time on training the processes to capable people who could replicate your brilliance and creativity!

Chick-fil-A did it. Every franchise has done it; that is what a franchise is. When you buy into a franchise, you are essentially buying a process road map to walk you step by step through how to make a hamburger, pick up garbage, unload a truck, change brake pads, or build websites. Franchises exist for each of those services and thousands more.

You may have no desire to franchise your business, but wouldn't it be great if others could *run* your business with the same clarity and focus that you run your business with?

It can happen.

You can do it.

See you at the top (Thanks, Zig)!

In 2017, a friend of mine who owns a brilliant dental clinic locally texted me and said, "You've got to read Chuck Blakeman's book *Making Money is Killing Your Business.*" Never one to turn away an excuse to dive into a book, I began listening to Blakeman's book in audio version and enjoyed until I came across an entire section Blakeman refers to as "Process Mapping."

If my memory is correct, I was doing yard work when I stopped and spoke audibly to no one in particular, "Yes!"

Blakeman wrote that "People don't buy quality; they buy consistency."

Throughout this important book, Blakeman walks through the progressive benefits of "process mapping."

A light bulb went off for me not only for our own Business On Purpose team, but also for the other heroic small businesses we have the privilege of serving. If we could build a one page, logical, color coded road map that anyone in the business could look at and get to every process in the business, cross-training, confusion, and chaos would be unnecessary.

Welcome to the master process road map. On this one magic document, you will record the title of every major process that makes your business work.

The process clarity and repetitious implementation will create a repeatable business that pushes you toward your vision while allowing you to consistently out your mission and is in line with your unique core values.

With this one document you will have built a curriculum for training that will make you feel like you are running a full-scale business university for your team. Training will become a hallmark of your small business. The product will become less and less the focus and training your team to deliver a great product will increase with habit and time.

Talk to business owner after business owner, and the one thing they will constantly preach is equipping and training their team. Talent grows as training grows, yet too many of us rely on "raw talent" and get burned in the end.

Give me world-class training with average talent who implements everyday over world-class talent and average training . . . every day.

The little-known secret is when you begin to offer world-class training to average talent, the talent will eventually rise to the training!

Let me show you a process road map that will buy you time for what matters most and get you off the treadmill!

Here are the basic elements of a simple process road map:

One document (we use the free Google Draw)

Roles with color codes

Systems aligned with the Org Chart

Every major process within the system

Color code processes (single point of accountability) and add any major supporting roles

Document process and link

Team Meetings, train, implement, repeat

This is a Master Process Road Map template that you can launch from.

Partners

CEO

Major System
- Sub-System
- Major Process
- Process
- Sub-Process
- Sub-Process
- Process
- Sub-Process

Major System
- Sub-System
- Major Process
- Process
- Sub-Process
- Sub-Process
- Sub-Process
- Process

Major System
- Sub-System
- Major Process
- Process
- Sub-Process
- Sub-Process
- Process
- Sub-Process

Major System
- Sub-System
- Major Process
- Process
- Sub-Process
- Sub-Process
- Sub-Process
- Process

LET YOUR BUSINESS BURN

This is an actual sample of the brilliantly executed Master Process Road Map from the game-changing Pearce Scott Architecture firm.

Your Master Process Road Map is a working document. Always updating, always reviewing, always training. Every person should have this printed out in front of them.

This is your business processes on one sheet of paper.

This is your narrow brilliance.

This is your offering to your world.

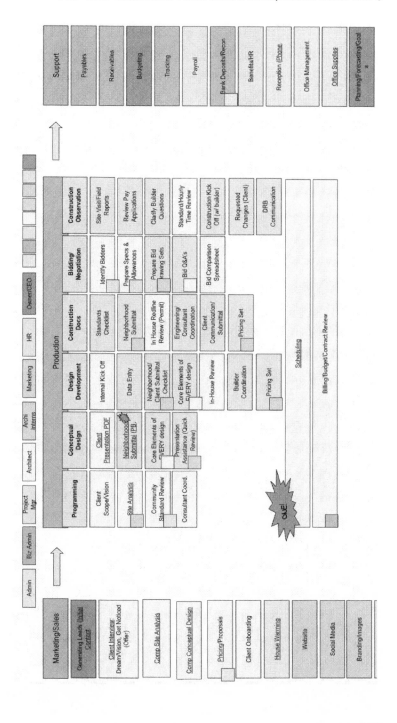

Step Three:
Building Your
Chaos-Conquering Team

ORGANIZATIONAL INFRASTRUCTURE:
Team Meetings and Huddles, Job Roles, Four Personalities,
Leader as Coach, Performance Reviews

Team Meetings

This text came in from one of my clients: "You've got to listen to Mulally." Mulally is a corporate turnaround leader.

Bryce Hoffman is a journalist who has spent a considerable amount of time covering stories within the auto industry. Before reading Hoffman's book *American Icon*, I had no idea of the media entourage that was assembled within earshot of the Big Three American automakers' home offices (General Motors, Chrysler, and Ford Motor Company).

Hoffman leveraged his relationships with Bill Ford (Chairman of Ford Motor Company) and former Ford CEO

Alan Mulally to draft a powerful memoir (*American Icon: Alan Mulally and the Fight To Save Ford Motor Company*) on the epic turnaround of the Ford Motor Company during the period of the Great Recession. Although the stories are gripping and quite gallant, the accumulation of highlights and dog ears in my copy of *America Icon* have less to do with the dramatic adventures and more to do with one particular theme that emerges throughout the narrative.

Ford was reported to have hit a wall, lost market share, and fell behind Toyota, which had assumed Ford's spot as the second largest automaker in the world. Conversations around bankruptcy, selling the company, and loss of stock value were commonplace in Ford's camp in the first decade of the twenty-first century. The company founded by the venerable patriarch Henry Ford was at risk of being sold outside of the family.

Enter Alan Mulally, a notable turnaround leader who had spent a career at Boeing after being inspired into aviation and engineering on the heels of John F. Kennedy's great moon-shot speech in 1962 (another powerful example of vision motivating an entire nation!). Hoffman relays how Mulally rose through the Boeing ranks over the '70s, '80s, and '90s. He had the opportunity to work on most of the major jetliner programs at Boeing leading up to his breakout role on the Boeing 777. At the time the 777 was among the most complicated jetliners, and it was a gamble that *had* to work for Boeing as they were staring down the face of global competition with its European rival Airbus Industrie.

It was in this role as general manager of the Boeing 777 program that Mulally began to embed a philosophy that he had learned from then Ford CEO Donald Peterson who, as Hoffman noted, was on Boeing's Board of Directors. Peterson and Mulally were able to connect, and Peterson suggested that Mulally study what Ford Motor Company was doing with a development program called "Team Taurus," an automobile design that kicked off in 1986 and would become one of Ford's iconic brands which was the best-selling car in America at that time.

In order to pull off a successful introduction of the Boeing 777, Hoffman notes on page 61 of *American Icon* that Mulally would have to "command a team of ten thousand and a supply chain that stretched over four continents." Mulally harkened back to some of the principles he learned from the "Team Taurus" project and created a plan of "enforced cooperation and transparency."

Under Mulally's leadership and the philosophies shaped in part by the leadership at Ford Motor Company, the Boeing 777 would become Boeing's most successful program to date.

Fast forward to September 2006 and Alan Mulally is now the new CEO of the iconic Ford Motor Company. The company was broken, in shambles, losing money, and the culture had leaked to a point of palpable toxicity. Mulally was brought in to turn Ford around from the outside the same way he had helped turn Boeing around from the inside.

The entire story that Hoffman shares throughout *American Icon* is a torrent of corporate rapids with few spots of respite and calm. The intensity both at Ford and throughout the automotive industry, including the massive United Auto Workers (UAW), is pressing and unrelenting.

There was a turning point in Hoffman's account that subtly caught my attention early and continued to reinforce its importance throughout. Hoffman tells of a story where two of Ford's directors are concerned that Mulally does not have the intention of hatcheting the "sacred cows" within the Ford Motor Company—those "untouchable" executives whose esteem and machismo has put everyone on notice against firing them and keeping those colleagues on edge.

Mulally revealed why he wasn't going to have to get rid of many people. Hoffman relays how Mulally then "responded by outlining his system of weekly meetings. He told them this approach enforced extreme accountability on a weekly basis and left no hiding place for anyone who was not entirely committed to executing his part of the business plan." Mulally went on to say, "It is likely that a lot of people at Ford are not used to that, and they will self-select out . . . I won't have to do it."

That is it? For a CEO who is going to come in to a broken, nepotism-riddled, legacy-obsessed company commanding a multimillion-dollar compensation plan? A "system of weekly meetings" is how you plan on turning this megalomaniacal ship around?

Throughout *American Icon* Hoffman reviews the now infamous weekly Business Plan Review (BPR) meetings that Mulally installed. Just like any good, repeatable system, there were elements that were published so everyone was on the same page with these important meetings.

The primary elements and principles that Hoffman lays out in *American Icon* of the the BPR meetings are:

Attendance: Every executive must be in attendance.

Presentation: Every executive must present his/her own data (may not have an assistant present). This required advanced preparation.

Time: Business unit leaders were allotted ten minutes for their presentations, and function leaders were allotted five minutes.

Slides: Preset slides with only the data points that the team needed to know for making decisions with each slide including a green, yellow, or red color code system to quickly understand progress toward a goal.

Hoffman revealed that these meetings took place every single week. During the Great Recession, the executive team began huddling daily and, in some cases, multiple times per day.

One other element of note that is now infamously tied

to the Mulally turnaround is, as Hoffman wrote, the use of a simple wallet card or "pocket manifesto" (pg. 247). On this wallet card was the Ford catchphrase, an abbreviated vision, and the expected behaviors. Team members would have a constant, repetitive reminder of what they were getting out of bed and coming to work for each day.

Could it really be that simplistic? A wallet card and a system of weekly team meetings?

Yes, with the understanding that *you* must add the effort and implementation.

What would a "system of weekly meetings" look and feel like in your small business? Let's tackle the elephant in the room right from the start. Most meetings really do stink. But they do not have to.

Most meetings are an *agenda-less rant* by multiple people looking to hit some kind of verbal home run hoping that the time set aside would have some value in the short term. But they do not have to be like this.

We are going to bring back the good old-fashioned team meeting and show you where it has restored confidence, clarity, and camaraderie in organizations from hospitals in Nigeria, architectural firms in Croatia, and contractor firms in the United States.

I can make you a promise. If you follow the template I am about to provide for you and adapt it to your culture and sustain it over time, I promise that your organization will not have a choice but to push toward the vision that you have drawn out!

Here is an important premise: if you do not have a regular means of communication, the vision has nowhere to go for implementation.

What we are about to lay out for you has been used in thousands of meetings over the last three years and adapted in many ways with some powerful results leading teams to finally unifying on the same page. There is one ingredient in all of this that is not magical, and it is available to anyone. More on that later.

First, we as organizational leaders need to be leading meetings that are on purpose. But how?

A meeting that is on purpose should have the following five marks:

Simple agenda. Every meeting will be complete with a written or printed agenda for every member to follow that highlights and prioritizes these specific elements.

First, start your meeting with one simple story about how someone on your team has lived out your *mission and values* from the past week. For instance, I might share that we had a potential client call, and when I talked with her about the need to implement the five bank accounts, she got off the phone and went straight to her bank to get them set up. She was living our unique core value of full implementation. And

163

we would celebrate that as a team just for a few seconds to set a powerful tone for our meeting.

BIG wins. Next, every meeting should include a brief time of sharing *BIG Wins*. The well-known founder of Strategic Coach Dan Sullivan uses the acronym BIG to remember to "Begin In Gratitude." BIG Wins are a time for each member of the meeting to share one brief win from the last week either personally or professionally.

BIG Wins work with the mission and values story in allowing the team to see behind the curtain and what is truly happening within the stories of people's real life. Business meetings tend to be a "drive in/drive out" situation with very little human connection. Chaos thrives where human connection is absent.

A BIG Win I shared recently with our team was how Ashley and I went out for one of our dates and were able to review our family vision and goals from the first six months of the year. We talked about how we were tracking great!

Accountability. After you set a powerful stage of human connection and story (only takes three to five minutes), then you check in for a time of *accountability* for last week's action items. This is where you review your accountability document (a spreadsheet or project management software of choice) to review progress of what was discussed last week.

STEP THREE: BUILDING YOUR CHAOS-CONQUERING TEAM

Chaos thrives when teams forget what they discussed last week and move on to newer fresher fires. Vision-centric, mission-driven leadership closes the book on old tasks before moving on to new tasks. If the tasks from last meeting have not been completed, assuming they really were that important, there is not much reason to move on to something new.

Business discussion. Once you have looked back to make sure everything is accounted for from the last team meeting, you can then move on to the business discussion. In our example before with Alan Mulally and the Ford Motor Company, this would be the Business Plan Review (BPR) section of the meeting. You can design this a few different ways. The simplest way up front is to go back to the systems road map and allow each system to be a bullet point of discussion in your weekly team meeting. Your business discussion items might look like this:

Administration

Sales

Operations

Marketing

For our Business On Purpose team, we allow our 12-week plan to be our business discussion outline so we can be laser focused. The 12-week plan is based on Brian Moran's book *The 12 Week Year* and is the simplest goal-setting and goal-implementing process we have seen that allows for only three goals per twelve weeks. As I am writing this section of the book, one of the three goals on our 12-week plan is to *finish this book!*

While the business items are still fresh on your mind, go immediately into the next section to write out your new action items that emerged from your business item discussion. Make sure you *document* each one of those action items with the task, the person of responsibility, the timeline, and any associated notes that may needed in order to complete the task. The number-one reason most team members think that meetings are a waste of time is right here, the failure to document and follow up on next step action items. Make this a priority, and chaos will run off.

Great meeting, *so far*. There is one more incredibly powerful element of your new team meeting structure that will change the game for your small business. This may be one of the most powerful and overlooked opportunities within the structure of the team meeting.

Recall back in the organizational road map section when I shared about CEO Thom Crosby and Pal's Sudden Service? Every team member at Pal's is said to invest a minimum of 150 hours of training and complete a sequence of two to three pop quizzes each month. Pal's has set a culture where the entire team feasts on a diet of regular training. Maybe that is why their turnover among assistant managers is *less than 2%.* In the fast food industry, of all places!

Training. During each weekly team meeting, you need to set aside the final ten minutes of the meeting to train your team on one process within the business. By training, we mean reviewing a top-of-mind process from your Master Process Road Map and making sure everyone understands the process or has a part in updating the process for understanding.

If you find that a process does not exist for a business discussion that you just had in the meeting, that training time is the perfect time to draw out that process as a team, and allow every relevant team member to have input while sharing the actual process in real time. The team can literally build it out in the meeting.

Marcus Lemonis is the CEO of Camping World and also headlines the CNBC television program "The Profit." In the show, he plays a hands-on investor who will assess a local small business and then decide to make an equity offer in the business. If the existing owners agree to the deal, then Lemonis always follows up with this one operational statement that usually catches the business owner off guard. Even though he may only be a minority equity holder, he says, "Once you cash this check, I am 100% in charge."

In order for you to develop a chaos-conquering habit of powerful team meetings, I would like to be 100% in charge of your team meetings for the next three months. That means you take everything that I have just shared about the weekly team meeting along with everything I am about to share with you regarding the principles of how you will lead your meeting—and you implement *all* of it. Don't leave anything out of the team meeting based on your excuse of, "Well, my business is different." No, it is not.

Deal? Remember, I want you to implement all of it.

Five Principles for Every Team Meeting

Here are the principles of the team meeting that will surround the agenda structure we just walked through.

First, every team meeting must have a defined leader who does not always have to be *the* "leader" (*read this HBR* article). Working for large multinational corporations granted opportunities to see who the obvious leader was in most rooms we entered. The empowering moments were when the known leader would entrust their leadership to another subordinate by allowing them to lead team meetings.

Growth-minded team members are constantly scanning the landscape for opportunities to grow in their leadership and take on new challenges, and the team meeting is an opportunity for that with built in oversight. When I attended corporate level meetings with the president of a multimillion-dollar company I would be taken back when someone else would open the meeting and begin running the entire team through the agenda. The president only spoke on issues that he felt needed additional clarity. The person "in charge" does not have to always be "in charge."

Next, every team meeting must have clear and defined participants. Cal Newport's transformative book *Deep Work* makes a thoughtful case for team members to carve out and *maintain* focus blocks of time necessary for what he classifies as deep work. Namely, "professional activities performed in a state of distraction-free concentration that push your cognitive capabilities to their limit. These efforts create new value, improve your skill, and are hard to replicate."

In a study published by the *University of California Irvine* researchers found that just 20 minutes of interrupted work directly correlated with a "significantly higher stress, frustration, workload, effort, and pressure." Many team members have their work interrupted by unnecessary or unproductive meetings. If a team member's role is not adding or drawing value from the meeting, then give them the gift of remaining within their uninterrupted deep work. Of course, every team member needs at least one meeting that they are a part of or else follow up on their work will be missing.

The third principle of your chaos suffocating team meetings is to understand a determined cost of the meeting in order to appreciate the time more. A few years ago, I was reading an article in the *Harvard Business Review* that was revealing the process of estimating the cost of a meeting. In the article the author(s) included a handy *Meeting Cost Calculator* that required input of the number of team members, the time allotted for the meeting, and the salary of each of those team members. Once submitted, out came a number that in most cases causes our clients to sit back and reconsider the value of their team meetings.

Every meeting has a cost, which is an investment into your business. Some of those meetings are providing a return on that investment while many are not. Your team meetings need to maximize the investment you are making into them with the implementation of the layout provided in the book.

The fourth principle of a great team meeting is to facilitate an atmosphere of predictability that will help root out the dreaded micromanager. Chaos loves a micromanager! I have yet to meet one person who is eager to wake up and sprint into an environment where every little detail is managed, and shame is distributed like cheap paddle-balls at an arcade.

Team members need predictability in order to have a constant mind of progress toward the vision. When you are driving down the interstate at high speeds, you are trusting in the predictability of the road engineers who have followed a predictable process so that your vehicle does not tail spin into a driving missile.

Predictability is substituted for chaos in the world of a small-business owner with thoughts like we need to keep them on edge so the innovation is always in full gear. No! Humans like predictability that creates stability for when unpredictable chaos actually *does* enter the building—and it always will.

We have created a model we call the seesaw of predictability to help diagnose whether you are prone to micromanagement. The seesaw has two sides of the fulcrum, time on one end, and questions on the other. Here is how it works.

TIME   QUESTIONS

If you ask a predictable question at an unpredictable time, you are micromanaging. For example, "Jessica, can you send me yesterday's sales numbers?" Sounds like a good question, unless you send it in a text on a Friday night at 11:30 P.M. You have asked a predictable question (sales numbers) at an unpredictable time (Friday night at 11:30 P.M.).

If you ask an unpredictable question asked at a predictable time, you are micromanaging. For example, you are sitting in your team meeting discussing sales numbers, and you ask Jessica to you send you Q1 sales numbers from nine years ago. You have asked an unpredictable question (Q1 sales numbers from nine years ago) at a predictable time (weekly team meeting).

If you ask a predictable question at a predictable time and place (like a regularly scheduled meeting), you are leading your team well. If you are in your weekly team meeting and you ask Jessica to send you yesterday's sales numbers, then you have reinforced predictability, punched chaos in the mouth, and empowered your team member to live out her job role.

The five principles that every purpose centered meeting should include: a defined agenda, a defined leader, a defined participant, a determined cost, and an atmosphere of predictability.

Five Things Every Team Meeting Should Avoid
Briefly, here are five things every purpose-centered meeting should avoid at all costs.

Chaos was beginning to lose its grip on society for a while, and then the technology revolution kicked into high gear. In full disclosure, I am thoroughly enjoying not writing this book on an antiquated typewriter but on a Mac with a simple document creator. I record episodes of My Business On Purpose podcast on my phone, and many of my coaching calls are completed virtually online from wherever I am. Technology is powerful, and I am leveraging it.

I have also had to declare authority over technology and ignore some of it. It is addictively distracting, as you are well aware.

First, the easiest and most justifiable way for chaos to knock you away from your powerful team meetings is with technology. Your team is there, but they are not really there. Avoid technology distractions at all costs. The team meeting is one hour of your week, so you can lay off the tech for one hour. Allow yourself the gift of making human connection in your team meetings and maximize that time.

Do something silly like create a special "Device Resort" somewhere in the office *outside* of the space where your meeting will be. Promise all meeting attendees that their devices will be pampered and well cared for while the device is resting.

Second, going back to the seesaw of predictability, make sure to avoid an atmosphere of unpredictability. Ask predictable questions during your team meeting. If you plan on dropping a surprise bomb in your meeting, think about preparing people individually in confidentiality.

Next, please do not cancel your team meetings. Remember, you have made them so repeatable and predictable because of your powerful meeting agenda that any team member can lead the meeting. Create a recurring time in your calendar and in the office Master Calendar (if one exists), and communicate to people that other things need to be scheduled *around* this meeting. The communication of your team is dependent on this meeting.

The one tool that can be used if a team meeting time will absolutely not work is to relocate the team meeting for that week to another time that works better. You can always reschedule, but please never cancel a team meeting, or chaos will come take residence in those empty seats.

Fourth, avoid getting off agenda. Chaos will continually try to flash shiny objects in the room so that you and the team will get off topic. Do not take the bait. Our Business On Purpose team has created a "future" section within our 12-week plan. If a new idea emerges within our team meeting, we add it to the "future" section and come back to it when it is time to build our next 12-week plan.

Another method of avoiding shiny objects in the team meeting is to create a good old-fashioned Parking Lot for any items of discussion that come up and are off the agenda. Do this especially if the business owner is in attendance—we are usually the worst offenders. You will need to forward any Parking Lot items to the next meeting or to a special time.

Finally, avoid being okay with a lack of implementation. Be consistent about reviewing and updating your action items throughout the entire meeting as items come up. Also, when you see a team member legitimately struggling to get his work completed, create a culture among the team that asks what can I do to help you get this done?

Chaos hates intentional conversation and encourages long pauses between meaningful team interaction. Be consistent with your team meetings. Follow the outline above so you and your entire team can press on to the vision story that you have laid out.

Job Roles

You cannot have a meeting without people, and you should never have people without job roles. The number-one headache we hear from the majority of heroic small-business owners revolves around one issue consistently: employees.

How do you find, keep, and grow talented, thoughtful, and mission-centered team members to help you drive toward the compelling vision story that you have for your business?

The owner of a $3 million landscaping company called me furious over his employee. "He just won't do the job the way that I want him to do it! I am sick of having to jump in myself and finish up his tasks. Why am I spending the money in the first place to hire him if I'm the one that's going to end up doing the work anyway?!"

After encouraging my client to take a deep breath, we began to walk through the situation. I asked a few simple questions, but one in particular led to a long pause, and I immediately knew the answer.

My question was, "Have you written out a job role for

this team member, and do you review it regularly so he knows exactly what is expected?" The pause happened here. After a few seconds, my client responded quietly, "Well, I told him three months ago about how to do this." There was no reason for me to add anything. He knew what was going on.

Chaos loves assumption and despises clearly and regularly communicated expectations.

For four years, my college roommate Gerrick Taylor and I had the opportunity to be a part of the University of South Carolina Division One varsity football team where we played in the competitive Southeastern Conference (SEC). Gerrick and I were *not* of similar athletic capabilities. He won lots of awards in high school for football, and I only played one year and had to lobby for a stupid letter from my coach. He was invited to be a part of the team whereas I lobbied my way in.

During those four years we traveled to small towns like Gainesville, Florida, and Knoxville, Tennessee, to compete against some of college football's greatest teams. Many of the players we would see on the field went on to play for years in the NFL.

Two of the standouts were Florida's Danny Werfel and Tennessee's Peyton Manning, and both were there all four years that we were there. We never beat either player in four years.

Imagine if Peyton Manning, likely one of the best three quarterbacks in NFL history and certainly the most legendary at Tennessee, reported to practice in Knoxville his first year and Head Coach Phillip Fulmer looked at him and said, "We want you to play quarterback," and then walked out of the room. Very little further instruction, no documented playbook, just a title of quarterback.

It would be reasonable for you to assume that Peyton Manning, having an incredibly successful high school career as a quarterback, should know how what a quarterback should do. It would be reasonable, but it would not be right.

Peyton Manning knew how to be a quarterback based on his talent, but he did *not* know how to be a quarterback at the University of Tennessee. In order to appropriately fit Peyton Manning's talent with the Tennessee opportunity, coaches worked endless hours to document and teach Peyton Manning and the hundred other players that would compete on Saturdays in the fall each year.

On a successful collegiate football team, every role is scripted, and every player knows exactly what is expected of him on every play.

As a deep snapper on special teams, the overwhelming majority of my plays were on fourth down, and yet it was clear what was expected of me on first through third downs—practice in preparation fourth down.

In the insightful book *The Score Takes Care of Itself,* Coach Bill Walsh is recorded as having documented *every* role on the San Francisco 49ers' football team. Bill Walsh even

wrote the phone script for the 49ers front desk reception-
ist. According to Walsh's book, the 49ers coaches "identified
thirty specific and separate physical skills, actions that every
offensive lineman needed to master in order to do his job at
the highest level . . . they were practiced relentlessly until
their execution at the highest level."

If you do not set the expected role for each of your team
members, they will have no choice but to make it up as they
go, and you are not allowed to get frustrated with them—
regardless of their talent.

Job roles are a must in every business for every team
member. From now on, please commit to never hire, fire,
promote, or pass judgement on a team member for whom
no clear job role exists. Chaos would love for you to keep
your team members in the dark and use excuses like, "It is
just stocking shelves; how hard can that be?" Put the excuses
in the trash can, set the time, and start building simple job
roles that will breathe life into your team members and into
your business.

To build simple job roles, all you need are a few elements.

First, every role is going to begin with the mission statement and the unique core values of your business right at the
top. Each team member needs to know that you are expect-
ing them to know and herald the mission and the values in
every aspect of their role.

After you have inserted the mission and the values, you

will then move down the job role and assign the first task and responsibility of the role. This task and responsibility will sound just a bit different on each role, but the meat of it is the same. It looks like this:

Single point of accountability for the day-to-day _____ of the business based on the

Vision

Mission

Values

Every role within your business must understand that it is positioned as the single point of accountability for something that happens each day. For instance, you may have one team member who is the "single point of accountability for the day-to-day *sales and marketing* of the business based on the vision, mission, and values."

The team member, through this job role is beginning to understand that the buck stops with them when it comes to this set of tasks, and every action should be aligned with the vision story, the mission statement, and the unique core values that you have worked hard to set out. That is why reviewing the vision story monthly and the mission and unique core values at every team meeting is so crucial. It is what makes your business airtight so every tool that you are building through this book has a place where it can be repeated for mastery.

Everything beyond point number one above will drill down on the various tasks existing with the specific role that you are working on. Each will look like this:

Big Bucket item needed for the role based on vision, mission, values and systems

- Process
- Process
- Process

To determine what the big bucket items will be for this section of the job role, ask what are two, three, or four major elements of responsibility for this role. You may have a role you are building in your administration system that will be handling some accounting tasks and process. You would answer the question with "They will generally be focused on billing, invoicing, and accounts receivable." It would be followed by a similar question for each of those three items (billing, invoicing, and accounts receivable). What are the two, three, or four major elements of responsibility for this task? This is how your role would begin to shape up based on those examples.

Two other sections that I recommend are a section for communication (*who* is this role responsible for communicating regularly with such as customers, vendors, the administration manager, etc.) and a section for other tasks because there are *always* other tasks—they still must be documented.

If you were to follow the examples above, your job role might look something like this:

Single point of accountability for day-to-day income management of the business based on the

> Vision
> Mission
> Values
> Billing
> Customer Database
> Data Entry
> Weekly Income Meeting
> Invoicing
> Customer Database
> Date Tracking
> Purchase Orders
> Rebates
> Accounts Receivable
> Data Entry
> Aging Reports
> Weekly Collections Meeting
> Bank Deposits

Communication

Vendors

Customers

Banker

Administrative Team

Operations Team

Weekly Team Meetings

Other Tasks

Weekly office supply inventory

Weekly office supply ordering

Initial meeting with Vendor Representatives

Finally, any good job role will have a title of the role at the top that will completely the fit the role itself. Do not be sucked into the lie that your roles have to sound like everyone else's role. Just because your friend who owns a nail salon has an office manager does not mean you need an office manager. When you draw out the role, you place the title last so it accurately describes what the role is.

Chaos wants you to create complex and overbearing job roles with details bursting from all sides, or chaos wants you to ignore job roles altogether.

Let's conquer chaos and build every job role that exists in your business based on the Systems and Organizational Road Maps which are deeply rooted in your powerful vision story.

You have invested time in building simple job roles, now let's build a simple plan for how you find the right people for the right roles that take you in the right direction toward your vision story.

Anxiety-Free Hiring

Small-business rosters are filled with underperforming talent. When we are working our way—many times too swiftly—through the mine-ladened waters of hiring, we are way too quick to hire and way too slow to train.

The phrase is "hire slow and fire fast," but why would we have any hesitation at all to fire if we know this person is a misfit for the role? People who do not fit the roles are usually miserable themselves and leave you frustrated and uneasy.

Hiring can also be expensive if poorly executed.

Hiring brings huge value to a business owner who wants to stop spending so much time putting out fires working in their business and enjoy the freedom of working in their business.

An innovative turnover cost calculator from Bonus.ly (*https://bonus.ly/cost-of-employee-turnover-calculator*) shows that losing one $45,000 annual salary team member to turnover for any reason will cost the company $23,271. That is significant and well worth any effort on the front end to find the right person for the right role at the right time.

I have a seven-step process that will bring clarity to your hiring and help you recruit the right people for the right roles.

Define the Gap

First, mind the gap. One of the deceptive tools of chaos is lead you to believe you need to hire someone when you may not. Or you may hire someone full-time when all you really need is someone part-time and remote.

We are quick to bring someone in as a desperation shot to fix an acute frustration, and we rarely pause to think about the massive consequence of the wrong person being in the wrong role at the wrong time. Before hiring anyone, make sure you see a real defined gap in your business.

When you think about your day, what are the items that deplete your energy? Make a list of those items and use that to help build a job role. Refer to the Delegation Road Map to get clarity on the gap that exists in your business.

Write the Job Role

Write out a job role as we have laid out for you in this book. Use a personality assessment and include the personality temperament or profile this role will need. The Business On Purpose team uses the DISC profile, and we have had the unique honor of taking over 600 people through the assessment to understand their profile.

184

The role needs to describe what *your* business needs and not what some other business has. Just because you are in the same industry does not mean you should have the same roles. Remember your business is a business based on your vision story and not on an industry standard. Just because ACME Co. down the street has a full-time controller, it does not necessarily mean that you need one.

Make the role description understandable and what you need based on the process I have laid out for you.

Remember to build your job role to be role first, people agnostic. You will rarely win in building a role around a person or a personality that you have in mind—that rarely works. Rockstars come with baggage, and you will likely spend more time managing the baggage than benefiting from the talent of the rockstar (of course there are rare exceptions).

The more clarity you can bring to a role, the more clarity it will bring for the person you eventually get to fill the role. It is the irony of building a people-focused culture; do not start with the people. Start with clarity of what you are asking the people to do.

Budget the Role

The magnetic Jesus was being followed by a crowd of people when he shared with them the seriousness of what was required of men and women who had elected to pursue him and his life.

After a strong introductory statement, he shared a construction metaphor, "Do not begin until you count the cost. For who would begin construction of a building without first calculating the cost to see if there is enough money to finish it? Otherwise, you might complete only the foundation before running out of money, and then everyone would laugh at you. They would say, 'There's the person who started that building and could not afford to finish it!'"[3]

Turnover costs in a small business easily exceed $20,000 per employee. Emotional labor is also required to work with another person. For these reasons, it is crucial that we spend just a few precious minutes walking through a simple budget for this role. You owe that time to your business, to your other team members, and to the new role that you are about to fill.

To work up a simple role budget, ask how much time and freedom this role will offer your business, and how this role will impact your revenue and margins.

A ratio that we have seen small-business owners use is a 1:3 or 1:4 ratio. You can ask a question with these ratios by asking if this new role will either directly generate three to four times the amount that we are compensating the role, or will this role indirectly free someone else up to generate three to four times the amount that we are compensating the role?"

We do not do break-even roles or a 1:1 ratio because we are running a business that will run a profit to fund the vision, mission, and unique core values that we have set apart.

Profit will never be achieved with a break-even mentality. Chaos loves a 1:1 ratio—we do not.

One more question to ask as you budget this role is will this role free up more of your time to work on the business and cut the anxiety of constantly working in your business? By asking that question, you will have more confidence in hiring the right people at the right time for the right role toward the right vision for the right compensation!

So, you have assessed the gap, written a clear and compelling role, and set a budget. Let's find the right person.

Intentional Recruiting

Living on the coast, we are used to seeing shrimp boats. Shrimp boats cast wide nets and catch lots of shrimp. They also catch lots of other things that they have to cull through in order to get to the good stuff. That is the challenge of casting a wide net. Let's fish with a fishing pole before we drop the wide nets and see if we can target a small list of individuals whose narrow brilliance may resonate with the role that we have thoughtfully built.

I asked one of our clients one time, "What is your criteria for hiring someone?"

His response was "A pulse." We only half-laughed at the time, but his hiring process has changed dramatically since. Just because someone is *available* to work does not mean they are the right fit for the role.

Here are the tools you need to begin working to attract the *right person for the right role at the right time*. Once you have written and reviewed your role, make a list of people you know who work within similar roles, or other business owners that you know who have similar roles in their business.

Reach out to those contacts and ask them, "I am looking to bring on a new team member who will be responsible for *these specific tasks*. Who do you know that I should talk to or may be a good fit for this role?" Of course, if you are talking to a fellow business owner, then reassure them that you are not going to hire their team member away!

Notice in the short script above I did not mention the title of the role but the specific "big bucket" tasks within the role. Start with role details and *not* title because your definition of a sales person is different than my definition of a sales person.

Share the *details* of the job role with those identified personal and business networks and be careful not to share the job role title.

For example, don't say, "I am looking for a bookkeeper." Instead ask, "Do you know of anyone with the skill sets needed to reconcile bank accounts, match receipts to expenses, etc.?"

To reinforce the point as you fish with one line instead of casting a wide net, leverage personal and business networks. Sales people tend to know other good sales people;

bookkeepers tend to know other bookkeepers. Start there. Instead of starting with a broadcast to the general population online or in a newspaper, go to a couple of other business owners and ask to speak to their bookkeeper (again promising that you will not hire them away). See who they know.

If some of your contacts bring you solid leads for the new role, then offer to incentivize those who help you. You were likely going to spend a few hundred bucks on a lead service anyway, and it is a great way to show your appreciation, excellence, and seriousness about finding the right fit for your vision. It is your business, so if you want to reserve a few hundred dollars as a thank you to the person who ends up referring your new hire (you can stage out the incentive payout), then do it. They will take it more seriously.

Stay laser focused. Even in a tight market talent is out there, and the right ones will *always* be more interested in a vision-driven, mission-centric, values-guided business than the majority who are not.

Do Your Homework

Once you have a few potential candidates (or even just one), you can begin to laser in on matching person to role. You can use these four tools to assist in compiling a comprehensive set of data points to make the decision. Unemotional data is important in this overly emotional process of finding a new team member to fit your culture.

Obviously, a phone discussion is a great first step that provides both you and your candidate an opportunity to discuss the job role and discover what questions or expectations they have. Asking general, open-ended questions about their general personality, values, and technical capabilities will usually allow you to get a good initial thought about their fit with the role. Here are some example questions that may help you get started:

- Personality—When you are at a get together of friends, how do you work the party? When you leave the party, how would you describe your energy level?
- Values—If you had six hours on a Saturday afternoon to do *whatever* you wanted, what would you do?
- Technical Capabilities—Tell me about how you have used (technical skill) in the past?
- Job Role—As you have reviewed the Job Role, what questions do you have for me?

Make sure you are taking notes the entire time and keeping those notes in a place you can constantly review even down the line. No phone call will be a waste of time because you will be able to learn and take away loads of information.

Assuming you feel this person would be one of your top three candidates, the next step would be to ask them to complete a personality profile/assessment (like the DISC) to further clarify if their personality is a fit for the role. They may have the skill set to perform the role, but will their personality fit with the rest of the team?

At companies around the world, more and more executive leaders and human resource professionals are spending more time evaluating soft skills (interpersonal communication, human connectedness, etc.) than they are in the technical skill set. Universities are beginning to push Humanities as a degree of choice realizing that technical skills sunset quickly and the real day-to-day innovation happens within the businesses which are uniquely setup for real-time training. The companies can train the technical and need team members who know how to be appropriately and beneficially be connected to other humans.

When you give someone a copy of the job role, it is like you are giving them a cheat sheet to prepare for the interview. We *assume* they are going to study the cheat sheet and pass the "open book" test with flying colors. You need to somehow receive *objective, unemotional* data to help make this important decision. You need to identify what makes this person really tick and which situational environments give them energy.

The personality profile gives objective insight to the subjective phone discussion. This is a great and simple both/and approach. Having personally read through and consulted on over 600 personality profiles, I believe in it so much that I will no longer give hiring advice without the client completing a profile first. It is a great objective set of information to complement the subjective work you are doing on the phone, with references, and in person. It should never be the only factor or the determining factor in final decision-making, but it is a powerful piece of the whole.

Continue your homework with old school reference checks. Call the references. Ninety percent of the time all will check out because the candidate has given you a list of what they hope are their best advocates. Occasionally, you may make the phone call and the "home run" on the other end may actually have that awkward pause that just saved you $16k—$25k in future turnover cost.

Call the references and ask them real questions around the candidate's values, their personality, and technical capabilities. Also, when you tell the candidate that you reached out to their references, you are letting them know up front that you have created a culture of diligence and action.

Your final piece of homework is to set up a test drive project. You can (in most cases) contract your candidate to do a test project. If you are looking for someone to help with bookkeeping, have them balance a mock bank account. If you are in need of someone to convert new customers, have them go on a sales call with you. If you are looking for a customer logistics person, have them make a delivery for you.

You can pay them for their time as a contractor and actually get a sense of how they are going to work. I know what you are thinking, "But they *can't* do a project for us in this type of business until they understand it." Wrong. Be creative. What do you need to know? Create a project, and pay them to do it one or two times. The insight will be invaluable.

If you really want to go to the next level in understanding a person, invite them and their spouse to dinner or out for an evening event. Invite them into a non-work situation where things are more relaxed, and you both can see more of a depth of what you are about to walk into.

The Live Interview Sequence

It is not until we are six steps into the process that we actually have a live sit-down interview or a series of live interviews.

There are a million ways to do these that are all well documented, so we will not spend much time here on it. Bottom line, pick one, be intentional, and implement.

Pulling the trigger for some is easy because they just want to get someone hired. For others, it could take months of uncertainty. Make this hiring process your own, and trust your process walking through it methodically . . . *do not skip steps*.

Develop a list of open-ended, situational questions in advance of your live meeting(s) (please do not try to do this on the fly) around these four categories:

- Your personal/business values
- Their personal motivation toward growth and development
- Human situational scenarios (tell a time when. . . .)
- Their technical skill (remember, technical skill can usually all be taught.. the values and personal motivations are usually more different to teach).

This section is intentionally short because I want to emphasize the *priority* of everything that leads up to the actual live interview, because they are what will determine the success of the live interview(s). If you skip the first five steps or do a halfway job, the data you receive from step six will be incomplete, and you will be making a risky hire. Chaos daydreams about risky hires.

Training Your New Hire

The seventh and final step of the hiring process transforms you from a doer in your business to a trainer for your business! You must see yourself as the Chief Training Officer of your small business, unless of course you have properly delegated that role.

I will remind you of Thom Crosby's statement on Pal's relentless training regimen. He was asked, 'What if you spend all this time and money on training and someone leaves?'" Crosby responded. "I ask them, 'What if we don't spend the time and money, and they stay?'"

The entire lifecycle of your new hire will rise and fall on the time, effort, and process you put into their initial training. On behalf of your new hire, please over-invest in initial training.

To prepare in bringing this new person on the team, make sure to take 30 minutes to sit down with their job role and build out a job role training plan. All you need to do is break the training down into a period of time (e.g. four weeks, five weeks, six weeks, etc.), and then take the priority tasks as they are found in their role and put those in week one. Then take the next level priority tasks and put those as training for week two.

Rinse and repeat depending on how much time you think it will take to train.

Answering these questions about initial training will make sure that everyone is on board to welcome the new team member:

- **Who** will be delivering the specific task training each day/week?
- **How much time** will each training task take?
- **What** delivery method will be used (e.g. video, live lecture, hands-on, etc.)?
- **How** will you evaluate mastery both now *and in the future?*

Your employees should always be in the mode of training so there is a stage for you to both hold them accountable to their actual performance and so you can constantly invest in the internal motivation to allow your team to wear the chaos-busting badge of honor. The easiest way to embed motivation and accountability into your business is through your weekly team meeting.

The team meetings that *really work* are rocket fuel to your small business.

Remember, if you will embed ten minutes per team meeting to focus on one of your business tasks for any role, your team will have received over eight hours of training in one calendar year with *no offsites, ropes courses, and cheesy ice breakers*.

These seven steps are crucial, and you will have the urge to shortcut them . . . **do not.**

Employment is not just a contractual transaction, it is a relationship. Relationships are emotional and complex. Do not underestimate the importance of taking your time.

Daily Huddles

Sometimes I'll reminisce on the first time that I ever snapped a football in a live football game. There were 80,000 rabid Tiger fans in the stands of the Baton Rouge LSU stadium. Rain was pouring down, and on the field I totted, this 195-pound kid who may have been more qualified to sell concessions than to snap a football to an awaiting punter.

I spent four years of my life playing football at the University of South Carolina with guys who were bigger, faster, and stronger. The game moved fast, and the playbook seemed endless. An average collegiate football game can see as many as 200 plays being run. Every one of those plays begins with a huddle. The huddle might be a group of guys in close proximity standing in a circle or scattered across the field. A huddle might even include coaches on the sideline communicating to the guys standing on the field.

The goal of the huddle is simple: make sure every player knows his assignment for the next play. The huddle is not to discuss a play that will happen 30 minutes later. That work is done during the weekly meetings prior to the game. Communication still must remain open throughout the game, and it must be quick and effective.

As we have already seen, chaos works hard to disrupt communication. If communication is disrupted, things begin to break down, and people begin to make it up as they go and get lost in their own agenda.

Without huddles, sports teams and their individual players would scatter in random chaos. With huddles, every team member moves in connected motion with the others.

You need to implement daily huddles. It is easy, and I will show you how.

Your daily huddle should be no more than five to ten minutes and in a rapid-fire format. This is not a time to check in on a person's personal challenges or deep dive into an issue. This is a quick go-around to make sure everyone knows what everyone else is doing and to uncover any questions or confusion that can be reconciled quickly.

Stand up. To begin daily huddles, set a time, a place, and a timer. The place can be live or virtual. The majority of our huddles and team meetings are completed remotely as our small team is literally all over the map. I encourage each team member to remain standing. Standing gives visual cues to everyone that this is a brief check-in so we know what plays we are running today.

Ask simple questions. I have read loads of books and learned from a legion of small-business owners about how they run their team meetings and huddles. We have collated five powerful statements and questions that will facilitate a quick and easy daily huddle. You will ask these of each person during each huddle.

- Question 1: What do you *see* as the most important task on your list today?
- Question 2: How can I help you with that?
- Statement 1: "Here is what I *see*. . . ."
- Question 3: "Does that make sense to you?"
- Statement 2: (Based on #3) "Here is what I need you to do . . ."

Three questions and two statements for a complete check-in, and they are asked rapid fire. The reason for the two statements is to make sure you have an opportunity to speak into their day as well. Your team will share with you the biggest thing on their plate from their perspective, but they might have missed something crucial. The "Here is what I see" and "Here is what I need you to do" speaks into that.

That is it. Daily huddles should be brief, and then you move on. The daily huddle is also a great destination for your nonnegotiable weekly schedule and for reminding each team member about their time availabilities, just in case someone needs them. It all works together, and it all works as a massively coordinated attack against chaos.

Performance Reviews

Ick. That's what most owners and team members think when they hear the dreaded phrase "performance review." As the owner, you might as well ask, "Do you want to spend loads of hours preparing for an uncomfortable discussion that will be totally worthless?" To the team member, you might as well ask, "Would you like for me to stick a hot poker in your ear?'"

Performance reviews are very rarely an actual review of performance and are more often than not a mismatched reflection of previous work with no clear outcomes nor forward-facing objectives. Are they even necessary?

I would like to propose a different type of review—an actual *review* of *performance*. Same words with a completely different mindset, method, and purpose.

You want your team to perform tasks for what the business needs—to accurately assess the team member and how they are doing relative to what the customer and the business needs them to do in their role and beyond.

Team members wants answers to their biggest question: "Am I doing what is needed and beyond, and what can I get even better at?"

Three tools will build a great culture of performance. These tools will not only be used on performance review day but every day, and two of them have already been built if you have followed the process laid out in this book.

The first tool is you need a job role. It is impossible, unpredictable, and unreasonable to evaluate performance on a role that does not exist in writing. Make sure that every team member in your business has a written job role, is clear on the role, is being regularly trained on the role, and is reminded of the role.

"But I showed them the role when they started!" Yes, and assuming that you are hiring humans, we all need to be reminded regularly—even you.

The second tool you will need to review performance is the short list of goals that you have worked on implementing.

Finally, you need a calendar in the form of your weekly schedule that you have already built.

That is it—a job role, your simple goals, and your weekly schedule. These three tools will play out to create a performance review that actually works and does not suck the life out of your days.

At least once per quarter, you (or the immediate manager) will sit down with the team member during performance review day and simple review tool number one, the job role. Of course tool number three, the calendar, is how you knew when and where this meeting would take place.

Just start walking through the role and give an honest assessment of what is working really well, and what you (and they) believe they can get better on. Bring the team member in on it. This will not be a "you vs. them" discussion; it will be an "us together" discussion. You are a team, and your goal is for the team member to do a great job with the role that has been created.

Once you have laid out that discussion and have come up with next steps, take out last quarters' 12-week plan and review performance in line with the actual tactics of the goals that you as a team have built. There is no guesswork with goals. They either completed the tactics or they did not. The performance will be clear.

When that is complete, pull out a blank 12-week plan template and build out three new goals for the next 12 weeks along with their tactics (see appendix). Build it out together and make sure that it in line with both their job role and the Vision of the business.

You have scheduled the time, reviewed the job role, reviewed last quarters' 12-week plan, and created next quarters' 12-week plan. You know their performance, and they know their performance.

Any gaps in performance will require you to take ownership of the disparity first. How will you ever coach the mindset of ownership if you are unwilling to own it yourself? Chaos would love for you to continue to ignore performance reviews and the value that comes with them to opt for disunity and confusion. Go ahead and schedule your date with clarity and set the time to review your team's performance.

We are rounding the final turn and about to head down the home stretch. It would be so easy to submit to chaos here as the RPM level on your business owner car is running at high levels, but continue pushing on and conquer chaos.

Step Four: Develop Your Chaos-Conquering Habits

American writer Will Durant wrote of habits, "We are what we repeatedly do. Excellence, then, is not an act, but a habit." Many small businesses are not process-driven because they do not consistently implement (*do*) repeatable and predictable processes.

Charles Duhigg's *The Power Of Habit* is a powerful overview of how and why we find ourselves living with the habits that drive us. Duhigg shares his Golden Rule of Habit Change: "You can't extinguish a bad habit, you can only change it."

In his book *The Coaching Habit*, Michael Stanier encourages us to consider others before ourselves when working through a new habit; "think less about what your habit can do for you, and more about how this new habit will help a person or people you care about."

Stanier goes on to lay out a three-part framework for

the hard work of changing a habit; a) identify the trigger, b) identify the old habit, c) define the new behavior.

If you want to build healthy habits within your small business, you are going to have to decide today, and tomorrow, and every day after that to *implement* these habits repeatedly, because you are what you repeatedly do.

If you repeatedly answer to chaos, put out fires, switch back and forth in multiple directions, then that is what you will be, a chaos responding organization.

Here are five repeatable habits that will set you and your small business up to make time for what matters most.

Habit One: Building and Documenting Process

He may be the most successful college football coach in history in the United States. Coach Nick Saban is known as a process-driven, hardnosed, focused, and effective coach.

As many times as he has been in a major game and/or won a major game, Saban is notorious for *not* pushing his players to focus on the major games. Instead, Saban subscribes and teaches something he calls "the process."

Saban declares within the process, "I do not want you to focus on the SEC Championship. I do not want you to focus on the National Championship. I want you to focus on the next play, the next film room session, the next workout . . . AND FINISH!"

There are multiple movements in sports. Multiple "finish lines" in any one given play. Running a successful small business is the act of crossing thousands of little finish lines, thousands of milestones on your way to the ultimate vision in your business.

In our vision story chapter, you learned that having a vision story is the foundational step of any business, family, or organization. But we have to drill down from there and figure out what steps are necessary to achieve that vision story.

Driving to a destination requires traveling one mile at a time. Driving your small business to its vision requires implementing one process at a time.

Those multiple, little "finish lines" are a collection of processes that have been identified, articulated, trained, and implemented with consistent accountability. The material restocking process, payables process, invoicing process, customer onboarding process, customer follow-up process, and the social media marketing process are just a few processes that will exist in most business. There are hundreds of others. But remember, one process at a time.

Developing a habit of building process in your business requires admitting that you need processes in your business.

Running around like a chicken with no head is draining. Are you are sick of constantly putting out fires? Perhaps you are frustrated with people doing halfway work on a timeline that does not coordinate with your business. Are you exhausted from the chaos?

In the spirit of author Michael Gerber, stop being a technician working *in* your business and choose to be a business owner working *on* your business. Decide right now that you will be a business that values and implements process. We were not designed to do it all.

Not even the great Jewish leader Moses could do it all. He looked at an entire nation and told God directly, "I cannot lead these people alone!" (Numbers 11:14). God granted him numerous helpers to manage most of the requests so he could focus on the biggest problems and not be exhausted from trying to do it all.

Until you come to a frank realization that you cannot juggle it all and maintain your health and sanity, you will not become a business owner who sets a culture of process. Decide right now. **I will begin systematically creating processes in my business for the sanity of my mind and the service of others.**

When you develop a process, it actually serves *others*. Others now get to leverage their own skill set instead of being bottlenecked with you. There are actually people in this world who would love to do what you do not love to do. Process facilitates that interaction.

Decide right now: I will create and implement processes, and through the delegation of those processes, I will have the opportunity to serve others by allowing them to live out their skill set and capability.

Remember your time is worth a minimum of $200 per hour. Every hour that is spent on something that someone else could do for $10, $20, or $30 an hour is a significant cost not only to your business, but also to your time. When you are doing the work of someone else, it not only costs you the difference of what your time is worth as a business owner, but it also costs you the actual time spent doing the task.

After you have opened up to the notion that you need processes in your business, it is then time for those processes to be created with places to collect the information that will inform those processes.

Your newly created Delegation Road Map is an information collection tool. These are the items that you wrote down and identified as "delegable" along including tasks that do not bring you a lot of energy after completing them. These are ideal processes to begin offloading.

Other information collection tools are your job roles. These roles are actually magical three-in-one roles that reveal where you want your team to play, provide a simple performance evaluation tool, and leverage a powerful training map for new processes that you can write out and train on. If the roles are the tasks you are asking a person to complete, then it makes for a great place to begin building process.

The job roles can help you think about the tasks that constantly frustrate you and zap your energy—responding to email, answering phone calls, taking out the trash, running to the bank, or paperwork.

How to capture a simple process. Identify one process right now that you wish you had drafted out. Creating a process that lasts will require you to figure out whom you will delegate a new process to, and how by asking, "*Whom* will I delegate this to and *how* will I document it?" Let's begin with the "how."

We will focus on two primary types of process documentation systems that we have found to work best. These are not overly fancy, so everyone can wrap their minds around them easily.

The most replicable and responsive of the two methods is video. Before you run away and say, "I don't know how to do video training." It is increasingly easy. Use that cool little camera on your phone, hit Record, and begin talking out the process *while you are actively working the process*. Upload the video to cloud storage, and a new process is born.

You are currently doing a task with your hands like taking out the trash, planting a shrub, fixing a tire, or stocking a shelf. Hit Record on your camera *while you are actively working the process*.

Much of your work might be right on the screen of a computer. If so, it is even easier. Download a plain screen capture software such as (at the time of this writing) Screenflow for Mac or Screencast-o-matic.com for any machine. There are also emerging cloud-based screen capture tools you should search for. We have been building processes with UseLoom.com. It is a game changer because there is no editing or uploading required (although we still recommend hosting your own videos).

Even if those tools are outdated at the time you are reading this book, there will always be some kind of screen-capture tool that you can leverage. Download it and use it. It is literally like having all of your future team members looking over your shoulder as you show them to do every element of the task.

Every time you record a training video, you have built a process that you may never have to train again—just let the video do it. We even have some small businesses that are building their own in-house video training schools in a Google Drive folder.

Go back and review Rory Vaden's 30x's principle where we were building your Delegation Road Map. Creating process is what gives a massive return on your hiring investment. Without creating processes, you are leaving a gaping hole for chaos to come in and begin unleashing its fury.

You might respond to this section on process building with frustration and ask, "Why can't they just do it the way I do it?!?!" Because we as business owners do not take the time to *teach the way we do it*.

Then we make statements like this, "Well it is just common sense . . . dang it, take the trash out!" What is common to you is not common to me.

You can either spend 150 minutes doing live training for a five-minute task each time it comes up, or you can do a video one time for five minutes, spend two minutes uploading it, one minute sending an email, and then a couple minutes a week following up. If they have questions about the process, all they have to do is click Rewind.

Process building and implementation together are a game changer for the business owner who has implemented this one strategy. Write down one process that you can video right now. Anything like bookkeeping or data entry done on a computer is perfect.

Another system of documentation that you can use is a simple written-out process. I am going to walk you through exactly how you do it.

Create a Process folder where you house all of your processes.

Create a new document with a straightforward and descriptive title of the process.

Start your process with the word "Trigger." Every process has a trigger, some time or event that kicks the process into motion.

Think like a curious eight-year-old who wants to know every detail.

Write out the three, four, or five (or more) major items of the process—these are Big Bucket items just like in your job role.

Then you will go underneath and create any details that offer more detailed description.

No doubt you are trying to find the time in your calendar to spend in drawing out these processes. Chaos will always lead you to believe you do not have the time. It is a lie. You are going to make the time using the "Systems Mindset." The next time you do a process, document it like it is the last time you will *ever* do it! The next time you do accounts payable, record it and delegate it. The next time you do customer data entry, record it and delegate it. The next time you repair a piece of machinery, record it and delegate it.

Based on your new team meeting structure and agenda, you should have a line item titled "Training." That is your time each week to either train on an existing process or to build out a new process for which there is a need to delegate.

When you implement process building and embed process building into your team, you build a culture of training. Your team will grow to expect it, and they will begin to conquer chaos.

Here is what the template looks like in developing a written process:

Example Process

Video Tutorial on How to Create A Business Process

Trigger (what action initiates this process?):

1. First step (once trigger happens, what is the first step in this process?)
   - Sub items within the first step
   - Sub items within the first step
   - Sub items within the first step

2. Next step (once trigger happens, what is the first step in this process?)
   - Sub items within the first step
   - Sub items within the first step

3. Next step (once trigger happens, what is the first step in this process?)
   - Sub items within the first step
   - Sub items within the first step

4. Next step (once trigger happens, what is the first step in this process?)
   - Sub items within the first step
   - Sub items within the first step

Managing hundreds of properties is a massive challenge. You must think through all of the logistics, maintenance, customer relationships, billing, invoicing, collections, owner payments, and so on.

Les has always led his business from a standpoint of overwhelm and endless hours of investment. He decided that chaos is not a viable long-term companion and began slowly building into Palm Property Management a mindset of process building and delegation.

Through a series of huddles, weekly team meetings, and radical implementation of his 12-week plan, Les has now trained the Palm team that process, delegation, implementation, and follow-up are the normal rhythms of business at Palm. The Palm office is loaded with color-coded white boards, digital tasks sheets, and folders with the workflows drawn out so each team member has clarity.

Palm is putting in the work to punch chaos in the mouth and create a business that serves a challenging market with consistency and predictability.

All business owners want to build processes. Les has taken action and is pushing through the muck to make it happen.

Habit Two: Metric Tracking

Key Metric Tracking

I am writing this section on another plane cruising at 503 mph about 36,000 feet somewhere just south of Iceland, and we have just over 2,500 miles until we land.

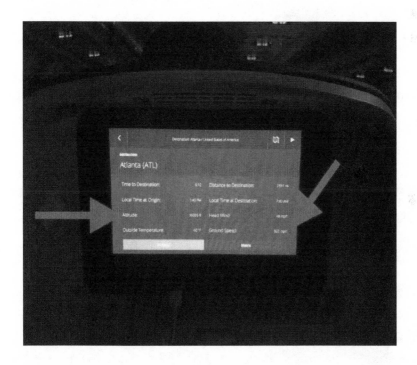

I love flying and always have. It gives me time to work on great projects like this. I am fascinated with the entire process.

LET YOUR BUSINESS BURN

As I have mentioned before, I love metaphors, and flying in an airplane with 300 lives and hundreds of thousands of dollars' worth of cargo makes for a book of metaphors.

When I board a plane, my first instinct is to usually look left and peek into the cockpit of the plane with gadgets and buttons everywhere. There are thousands of them with manuals to explain what to do a variety of situations.

Never have I flown a route where the pilot ran outside and started the jet by hand, ran to the front of the plane and turned the front wheel by hand as it is taxiing down the runway, then climbed on the fuselage back to the wings to manually make the flaps go down at the perfect pitch, and then go back to the tail wing to make sure that we could maneuver right or left at the appropriate time.

Silly as it sounds, this is how many of us try to run the business side of our organization. Running to open the doors, post on social media, send the invoices, collect payments and run them to the bank, design projects, bid projects, take out the trash, perform regular maintenance, and on and on.

Aviation realized that an immediate bottleneck to the flight experience was systematizing everything. The pilot(s) needed one geographical location from which to run every single shift, maneuver, turn, and assessment. The cockpit is a powerful design and is something that you as the leader can mimic and emulate. Pilots sit in one seat and gather information in real time from a well-designed and well-built dashboard.

As we continue to have the privilege of working with small-business heroes just like you, we continue to refine a dashboard of information that can allow you to continually monitor the health of the business which directly affects every single stakeholder impacted by the business.

We like to build the cockpit dashboard in stages in the same way that a small Cesna 172 has a more simplified feedback dashboard than the massive Airbus 380, so make sure to spend some time customizing your dashboard with the stock that we are about to provide, based on your unique situation.

You have already built out the five Bank Accounts that serve as your Level One Dashboard. As we build your Level Two Dashboard, we will build it out according to the ABCs of business and will want it to be as "metric" as possible. Each line of your dashboard is essentially asking a question. The "payables received" line is asking the question, "How much do we owe?" The "receivables outstanding" line is asking, "How much do others owe us?"

Accounts. First, we will start with the "A" of Accounts. If you do not know your accounts, then you do not know the full scope of your business. Chaos lies; numbers do not.

As you look at each account from the "A" section, here are the questions that each line will answer for you:

- All Income—how much total revenue have we received since our last account distribution?
- Profit—how much do we have in cash that is free and clear to use as we please?
- Owner's Compensation—how long can our family eat without bringing in another dollar?
- Tax—how much can I pay in government tax if they were to call right now?
- Operating Expense—how long can we run our business if we did not bring in another dollar?

Imagine the mental and emotional freedom you would have if we stopped the dashboard there and reviewed those numbers on a weekly, or every-other-weekly basis. If you can answer these questions, then you are in the serious minority of small-business owners.

Bookkeeping. For many entrepreneurs and owners, the "B" in bookkeeping means "the BANE of their existence."

The only thing more challenging than the books may be working with a challenging customer or team member. To keep it simple, you will need some sort of system for basic bookkeeping whether it be a software or a person. Do not try to save money and do this yourself.

Delegate this into capable hands sooner rather than later. This will eat your billable time fast—and bookkeeping is *always* hungry! Because you already have your "Income" account in the previous section, we will not double up here, and instead we'll call you to the "QARPET" with your bookkeeping. Here are the sections of the bookkeeping section and what clarity each will offer you and your team.

Quarterly Taxes Paid—
making sure you do not go to jail!

Amount Invoiced—
snapshot of what should be coming down the road.

Receivables Outstanding—
amount that you need to have a strategy to go get . . . in some situations, this may be the fastest income generator you have.

Payables Outstanding—
subtract this from the amount sitting in your Operating Expense account and viola, you know how much cash the business *actually* has after everything is paid.

Expenses Categorized—
this is more of a yes/no or a pass/fail metric. Getting behind on categorizing your expenses is easy to do, and super frustrating to have to go back and do!

Total Expenses—
this will serve as a barometer of your spending to see if there are some dips, spikes, and general fluctuations . . . again helping you see a trend so you can make powerful decisions!

LET YOUR BUSINESS BURN

Customers. If you do not have customers, you do not have a business. We finish the Level Two Dashboard with a focus on tracking our customer engagement. Sorry, no cool acronym for this one like calling you on the QARPET—but it is pretty straightforward.

We have left each line within the template in the customer section intentionally vague in terms of the metric you will use as the answer to each one of these questions. You will spend some time customizing the rows to your specific business using the categories below as a guide. Here are the sections of the customer section and what question each will answer you and your team.

> Marketing—what are we doing to make the right
>> people aware of our mission and our offerings?
> Leads—who and how many are showing interest
>> to our marketing?
> Conversion—who is both purchasing and re-purchasing our services? This is the number of new
>> customers or repeat customers.
> Product/Service Delivery—this will be some measure of quality control that you can define. For
>> instance, in our business, it is the percentage
>> of coaching engagements followed up with
>> our entire follow-up process (notes, follow-up
>> email sent, reminder for next meeting, etc.).

220

Follow Up—again, set a metric of what follow-up looks like for you and begin to track it.

Notice in our ABCs that we do not have a section specific to tracking the team or to the product. Instead we have embedded both subtly in the "Customer" section. Your team performance will be on display in each one of these questions, and your product will be reviewed in the last two points of "Product/Service Delivery" and the "Follow-Up" line. Again, customize these to your business so you are tracking the right metrics.

We get asked, "What is the right frequency for reporting and reviewing your dashboard?" To begin, we really do push for weekly or every-other-weekly reporting so a rigorous habit can be established in a powerful way.

You have heard it before: what gets measured get done. If you want to fly level at 30,000 feet and 200 MPH, then review your dashboard on a regular basis.

Others have asked, "How do we remember to look at our dashboard?" Do not try to do it from memory. Instead embed it as a line item in the business discussion section of your team meeting.

Your team meeting will be like an IV port when you go to the hospital. One port, and you can push all sorts of drugs, vitamins and fluids. Same goes for the weekly team meeting. One place where you can review everything that you are working so hard to build—12-week plan, mission, values, systems, training, and progress. Go embed it into your team meeting agenda right now.

One final tip. To know what metrics to use when filling out your dashboard, ask what metric you can pull out that will provide useful information to push you toward your vision. The "Accounts" and the "Bookkeeping" section are straightforward; those will be populated with the actual numbers from your bank accounts and from your bookkeeping software.

Having these numbers in one place will help you spend more time making great decisions based on accurate information rather spending all of your time haphazardly hunting for the data and then trying to join it together in order to make sense of it all.

Once the metrics are in place, do not let any one number ruin your day or make you think you have won. We are always more interested in using this dashboard as a barometer in building the habit of implementation instead of a fly-by-night strategy that you will do for a couple of meetings and then forget about.

This is a template overview of a Level Two Dashboard that you can implement.

		January					February	
	1/2/2017	1/9/2017	1/16/2017	1/23/2017	1/30/2017	2/6/2017	2/13/2017	2/…
Accounts								
All Income								
Profit* (Qtrly Draw in Green)								
Owner's Compensation								
Tax								
Operating Expense								
Bookkeeping								
Quarterly Taxes*								
Amount Invoiced								
Receivables Outstanding								
0-30 days								
30-60 days								
60-90 days								
over 90 days								
Payables Outstanding								
Expenses Categorized								
Total Expense								
Customer (customize)								
Marketing								
Leads								
Conversions								
Product Delivery								
Follow Up								

LET YOUR BUSINESS BURN

Chaos would be delighted to see you read through this section and ignore it to move on to something that feels a bit more urgent. Chaos is wrong—this is what is important now, and the final habit will serve as a whimsical way to reinforce the habits that you are building.

Habit Three: Implementing Goals with the 12-Week Plan

I could pepper you with a list of quotes, from here to the moon, about goals and goal-setting like "Setting goals is the first step in turning the invisible into the visible" from Tony Robbins, or "Think little goals and expect little achievements. Think big goals and win big success" from David J. Schwartz.

Or maybe this thought from Earl Nightingale, "People with goals succeed because they know where they're going."

And what goal discussion is complete without mentioning the master of goal-setting and sales motivation *Zig Ziglar* who lays out the seven steps to goal-setting . . .

1. State the Goal
2. Set A Deadline
3. Identify the Obstacles
4. Identify the People, Groups, and Organizations that Can Assist
5. List the Benefits of Achieving the Goal
6. List the Skills You Need to Acquire to Attain the Goal
7. Develop A Plan

Of course, the mother of all goal-setting methodologies is the S.M.A.R.T. acronym; specific, measurable, attainable, relevant, and time-bound.

Regardless of the method you use, we are most interested in the principle of identifying and implementing.

We have drawn our template and this idea from Brian Moran's book *The 12 Week Year*, which resets the business mind to see a full year of business in 12-week terms.

The pace of life is at a *dead sprint* so 12 weeks makes a lot of sense as compared to 12 months. Goal-setting five years out is almost irrelevant because so much changes within five years. Notice I did not say that your *vision story* five years out is irrelevant, just the goal-setting.

I will never forget our overwhelming zeal when we saw one of our children walk for the first time. Our child had learned how to literally put *one foot in front* of the other. That is it, right foot, wobble, left foot, wobble, right foot, repeat, and then . . . WHAM! It was a live metaphor of progress. She was learning the basic motion of all human progress, which is to take the next step.

What is completion; what is progress? What is forward movement in an organization, in a team, in life if it is not a collection of single steps toward and end line? Take any skill or task in life like dunking a basketball, flying a plane, becoming a world-class soccer player, building a bridge, or remodeling a kitchen. In order to complete the goal, you simply line out each individual step and then right foot, left foot, and repeat.

I played one year of high school football and was honestly not very good at it. When I got to the University of South Carolina, something inside told me it would be a great idea to try out for the football team.

For the next four years, I had the privilege to be a member of the team and earn a scholarship as a deep snapper after two years. This picture is actually the first time that I had ever snapped a football in a live game.

1994 South Carolina @ LSU Full Game Part1

People still ask how I did it. I put one foot in front of the other. I ran, snapped, worked out, snapped, slept, snapped, ran some more, snapped, lifted, snapped, met with coaches, snapped. Deep snapping was pretty much all I thought about from time I decided to pursue it until I actually put on a real game jersey to play Georgia at *Williams-Brice* in 1994. I was an overnight success, and it only took me nine months of total, all-in focus and relentless naivete to get there. For nine months, the *stadium* was empty . . . crickets. Nobody cared. Put one foot in front of the other. Do what it takes, and you'll experience more success.

The completion of a goal is a focused collection of steps in the same direction. A collection of purposeful and completed goals will take you to your defined Vision Story.

Collection of steps = Goal
Collection of goals = Vision

Moran explains brilliantly why the psychology of 12 weeks is so important in getting the right things done. If you set 12-week goals and review them every day and are non-negotiable about pull through, then you have the thirteenth week to review and recalibrate for the next 12 weeks.

We have used this method for the last couple of years, and the focus has been irreplaceable. We have been asked to run team meetings for *other* heroic small-business owners, and we build and hold them accountable using the 12-week plan. The results are clear.

Results of the 12-week plan can lead to a realization that the goal you wrote is actually *not* a fit. You only know that because you took the time to write it out and track it relentlessly for a period of time.

228

Results of the 12-week plan can also be exactly what you hoped they would be. This allows you to feel the power of accomplishment and that healthy addictive impulse encouraging you to build out the next 12-week plan and continue this habit of health and progress.

Assume you have your one-year vision story document. You will see immediately that four 12-week plans will be necessary to install throughout the duration to push toward your vision story. Since there are 52 weeks in a year, each 12-week period is allotted a thirteenth week that is used for a one-week retool between each 12-week plan. It is used for drafting great clarity on what needs to be accomplished for the next 12 weeks.

Our interest lies not in the method you use for goal-setting but in the implementation of your method. For our purposes, I will walk you through each step of creating a simple 12-week plan the way we do at Business On Purpose.

How to Build Your 12-week Plan

We have adapted a 12-week plan template from Brian Moran's book, and it is found below. As you work through the document, follow these steps.

First, write out the end date of your 12-week plan. Setting dates for your goals is a powerful and sobering motivator.

Next, you may have no more than three major goals. We tend to "over-goal" ourselves, and by the time it comes to implement and account for our implementation, we have forgotten what we are to implement. To pick your three goals, go back and review your vision story and determine the three most relevant steps that need to be implemented over the next 12 weeks in order to push you toward the Vision Story. Write those down in general terms, but do not be too specific yet.

Moran define goals as *outcomes* and defines tactics as *actions*. Your outcomes can be more general because your actions will be very specific.

Copy the goals that you have written out at the top and paste each goal in the first, second, or third goal windows below. The goal windows will serve as holding places for the actions you are about to write.

Moving down the 12-week plan template, each goal should have multiple tactics. The definition of a tactic is "an action or strategy carefully planned to achieve a specific end" and will be oriented for clear action. What are the individual and detailed steps that we need to do to cross the finish line of this goal? There should be multiple tactics.

If you are familiar with the S.M.A.R.T. acronym (specific, measurable, attainable, relevant, and time-bound), this is where you would apply that filter. Write down as many as it will take to get to the goal. Be overly specific.

Every tactic should be trained and tracked each week, preferably during the weekly team meeting that you have already set up. Train the tactic during the team meeting when it is assigned and track it each additional week with continual training as necessary.

Your team meeting is home base for your 12-week plan. Do not feel the need to create a separate meeting to follow up on your 12-week Plan. Embed it into the existing team meeting agenda that you have already built, if you took the time to build out your team meeting structure.

I can see chaos in the corner of the room pouting like a spoiled baby. Does that not feel great?

Here is a brief example of what a 12-week plan might look like.

12 Week Goals
For the term ending Sept. 30, 20XX we will… 1. Complete all Sales Training Modules 2. Onboard new Ops Manager 3. Create A Culture Of Learning

Goal 1: Complete all Sales Training Modules	Tracking
Tactics	
Block out every Tuesday morning for script writing	
Create and send training video on slide creation to VA	
Write out four module scripts: • Master Sales Workflow • Objection Handling • Sales Call Follow Up process • Lead Nurture	
Get VA to make slides for scripts	
Record Audio for each script	
Send audio/script/slides to VA for final video	
Upload videos	
Embed Videos into Team Training	

Goal 2: Onboard new Ops Manager	Tracking

Full disclosure on building your 12-week plan: it is not easy, and there is no autopilot solution for this. Put in the work over time, and it will become a powerful habit.

Schedule it and sit down with the template and think through that important question, "What are the three most important steps that need to be taken over the next 12 weeks in order to push us toward the vision story?"

STEP FOUR: DEVELOP YOUR CHAOS-CONQUERING HABITS

It takes time and thought, and when you get to the end of that first 12 weeks, you realize that you are three steps closer to your vision story than you were 12 weeks ago, and you know they are purposeful steps. They will not be haphazard, in vain, or just a guess.

Your habits are growing and are causing chaos some real nervous moments, but chaos has an ace up its sleeve: money.

Habit Four: Simple Budgeting

"It may just be better if you closed this business down and got hired as an employee somewhere." That was the wisdom that I gave Katie, a heroic small-business owner, after we uncovered that she was pocketing about $32,000 in salary and drawing compensation from working full-time in her bookkeeping firm.

Another client was in a similar situation. Clint had been operating his respectable architecture firm in North Carolina for 24 years. Clint's work speaks for itself and the process of how he serves his clients and empowers his team is admired and modeled in other firms. We sat down to review his numbers and realized that although he was bringing home an average salary, he had absolutely no margin for 24 years. Clint even made the comment to me over dinner one evening, "I've been running a non-profit for 24 years."

Katie and Clint are normal small-business owners. It is the norm for heroic small-business owners to *not* know their numbers. It is the norm for heroic small-business owners to *not* know their overhead, cost of goods percentage, or marketing spend.

It is the norm for an employee to ask the owner, "Hey, we really need (insert new software/tool/equipment here), can we get it?" And it is the norm for the heroic small-business owner to look at their bank account, ensure there is some money in there, and then give the green light for the employee's request.

The norm is *not* what we are shooting for as we liberate heroic small-business owners from chaos. As you have seen throughout this book, it is not that challenging to beat the norm and to not just be a product practitioner in your business. It is just as viable to *own* your business by owning your numbers.

This entire section would not have existed if not for a shrewd architect from Norfolk, Virginia. Mel Price, her husband Peter, and business partner Thom along with a growing team have built Work Program Architects into a firm that "strengthens community through design process."

We were interacting on a virtual coaching call for the Architect Firm Freedom Formula (AFF), a game-changing coaching program that I have the privilege of leading with world-class founder of the Business Of Architecture platform Enoch Sears. In the middle of our call, Mel asked bluntly and boldly, "How do we do a simple budget that gives us what we need without all the nonsense?"

My response was brilliant and noteworthy:

"Umm . . ."

Mel was right. She and every other architect and heroic small-business owner needed an easy way to develop a budget, leading us to question the purpose of a budget within the life of a heroic small-business owner.

Studying the utility of the word "budget," I found it surprising that the word was barely used until the early 1900s and has grown since. The word is a remnant of the *old French* (as opposed to Modern French) word *bouge* which means "leather bag."

It is as if Mel was asking to have a defined "bag" of money so that when her team was requesting resources for various spending, they knew how much was "in the bag," and in what compartments that money was remaining in.

Creating a budget is akin to creating a compartmentalized bag of preset funds that can be spent on the right things, at the right time, and *for the right purpose*.

Do not gloss over the last phrase: for the right purpose. Principles do exist in setting a budget that all heroic small-business owners will do well to follow, and after walking through this book you are perfectly placed to get started on a simple budget.

Looking forward. A simple and well-built budget will take a forward-gazing future look toward the vision of the business. A well-built budget is being spent on items that are steering the business toward the vision, in contrast to haphazard and emotional spending. A budget will have line items and categorizations that push you and the business toward the vision. If a category does not align with a healthy vision, it is removed from the budget.

Looking back. A simple and well-built budget will take a backward-gazing historic look toward the previous spending of the business. Starting a budget from scratch without looking at prior spending is akin to an amnesia-riddled pilot learning how to fly a plane every time she climbs into a cockpit. That is not a plane you want to be on. The quickest way to look at past spending is to run a profit and loss report from prior years making sure that the expense categories are visible.

Scheduling time. The third filter for a simple and well-built budget is setting aside the appropriate time to build your budget. Do not rush through it. Do not take all week, either. Block no more than one to two hours of time to review your vision and your previous profit and loss reports and project what you *think* you might need in each category in order to hit your near term goals (see 12-Week Plan module) *and* your long-term vision. Budgeting is not a perfect science.

Write it down. The final step in developing a simple and well-built budget is to write down numbers in every category. There is not a magic formula, but there *is* a helpful formula— create a clean budget sheet with the categories you normally use and the numbers zeroed out.

With your clean budget sheet, print out and use last year's percentages based on this year's revenue goals. To find the percentage, divide the expense number into the total revenue number.

If you showed a revenue of $1,000,000 and spent $800,000 in total expenses, you should have a net profit of $200,000. If you spent $400,000 of your expenses on payroll, then your payroll expense percentage will be 50% of total expenses.

Multiply *this year's* targeted expenses by 40% and that will give you a number to start with. Ask yourself ifs this what it is going to take to cover payroll this year with your new target revenue and expense number.

You will rinse and repeat the exercise all the way down your budget, both in the income section with any expected or projected income you are shooting for this year, and all of the expense categories.

Payroll taxes are likely to be included your profit and loss statement, but typically your business taxes will not be included. This is why setting up your five bank accounts is so important (see section on five bank accounts).

If you do not have accounting software categorized out and running these reports, it will serve you well to begin using an uncomplicated software too. Decide which brand you want to buy and let the purchase be one of the first processes that you initiate and delegate.

When you have these numbers plugged in, you are almost there. It is now time to embed these into your day-to-day life by setting up a once per month touchpoint to review your budget and update as needed based on increase or decrease in expected revenue.

You should also share your budget with your bookkeeper and/or financial professional so you can get their insight from outside of your business. And when asked, hey, can we buy this, you will respond every time with, "Does it fit our vision, mission, values, and do we have it allocated in the budget, and does it match up with cash in our operating expense account?"

That feeling is empowering! Chaos is sick to its stomach over this. A simple budget will make you feel like you *own* the business, like someone who is stewarding resources well and setting your team up for healthy, long-term success toward your vision.

Unicorn Habit: Implementation

The flow of business can feel stale and mundane. When Jesse and Emily Cole brought their idea of a business done differently to Savannah, Georgia in 2016, it altered the narrative of the city.

Imagine paying to attend a minor league baseball game during summer break. You know what to expect: dollar hot dog night, cheap hat giveaways, and small children racing around the bases between innings just barely beating the mascot to home plate. It is cheap entertainment, and spectators have low expectations that are typically met.

Summers in Savannah are different.

You cannot get tickets to tonight's minor league baseball game for the Savannah Bananas. They have been sold out for weeks. Every home game for the past two seasons has been a complete sell out. To heighten your curiosity, when you show up to a game, you realize that you are not even watching minor league baseball. The Savannah Bananas are members of a wooden bat collegiate league where it is illegal to pay players. As a paying attendee, you are watching amateurs play . . . and breakdance.

During a garden-variety home baseball game in Savannah, you will watch the entire team gather around a three-month-old baby at home plate, kneel, and raise their hands in admiration as the theme song to The Lion King blares over the loudspeakers.

You will watch the first base coach break out into a choreographed pop dance in between pitches. Players are walking outside the ballpark welcoming guests and signing autographs. Humans dressed as penguins are politely guiding attendees to convenient parking spots.

Individuals and news outlets around the world have tried to crack the magic code of what Jesse, Emily, and their young team of Bananas have been doing to see this level of success. It is not magic, although many people do claim to sell pixie dust that will give you amazing results.

If you were to scroll social media right now (please do not) you will run across someone who will guarantee life-altering money if you will just buy their system.

STOP!

Stop believing that success is a result of magic and happenstance. Stop believing that you can just show up and money will begin depositing itself into your bank account. Stop believing that you can jump out of an airplane without a parachute and gracefully land on your own two feet. Stop believing that you can focus on your product, neglect everything else, and your business will be healthy.

Humans who eat a steady diet of McDonalds, do not exercise, smoke two packs a day, and binge watch streaming movies are not healthy. If those are your habits, then stop complaining when feeling like trash.

Having some fun with this idea of finding the magic unicorn for small businesses, we decided to crown the mascot for Business On Purpose. The beach towel that Ashley found at the local store with a print of a unicorn riding a bicycle, much like a banana, really does make an impression.

We chose to name our mascot with an ironically appropriate name intending to declare that conquering chaos is *not* a result of magic or luck or wishful dreaming.

Our unicorn mascot is named Implementation.

How did Jesse and Emily build a small-town castaway baseball team empire? Implementation.

How did Ryan and Tiffany create a predictable and convenient system for Real Estate closings that serves their local community in a powerful way? Implementation.

How did Pearce, Maggie, and Allison build an Architecture firm that draws life and forms a community worth living in? Implementation.

How did Justin build an Exteriors Company that implores team members to grow, develop, learn, and share? Implementation.

Chaos is selling you a bill of goods that magic, luck, and silver bullets really do exist. The only unicorn we have seen work and stampede chaos is Implementation.

Let those little chaos fires in your business burn. They

will eventually starve of oxygen. Instead, build a business that serves, equips, loves, sees, hears, and understands. Be a courageous small business pioneer . . . a hero . . . and come ride the unicorn named Implementation.

APPENDIX
FROM ME TO YOU

Vision Story

"Write the Vision down so those that read it may RUN!" - God to Habakkuk

*"Your Vision **story** is a detailed snapshot of the future of your business"*

Term (months/years)	•

Family/Freedom	• Family/Friends
	   ○
	   ○
	   ○
	
	• Freedom
	   ○

Financials	• Current:
	   ○ Profit -
	   ○ Total Revenue -
	   ○ Total Expenses -
	
	• Future/Goal:
	   ○ Profit -
	   ○ Total revenue -
	   ○ Total expenses -

Product/ Services (see financial section)	• Existing
	   ○
	   ○
	   ○
	• Future
	   ○
	   ○
	   ○

*Reminder — this will NEVER be 100% complete. Just keep revisiting and tweaking.

Mission Statement Worksheet

"What drives you out of bed in the morning?!"
Top 12 Keywords
(choose 12 from the highlighted words on your Vision Story)

Mission Statement Attempts
note - look for rich words of imagery with double meaning, should be no more than 15 words in length

1	We exist to...
2	
3	
4	
5	
6	
7	
8	
9	
10	

Unique Core Values Worksheet

"Unique Core Values are the curbs along the road to your vision"

Keywords From Vision Story

Unique Core Values

	Value	Definition
1		
2		
3		
4		
5		
6		
7		
8		
9		

Five Bank Accounts

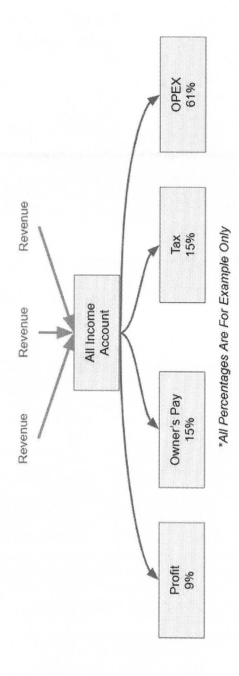

Revenue

Revenue

Revenue

Revenue

All Income Account

Profit
9%

Owner's Pay
15%

Tax
15%

OPEX
61%

*All Percentages Are For Example Only

Adapted From "Profit First" By Mike Michalowicz

Weekly Schedule

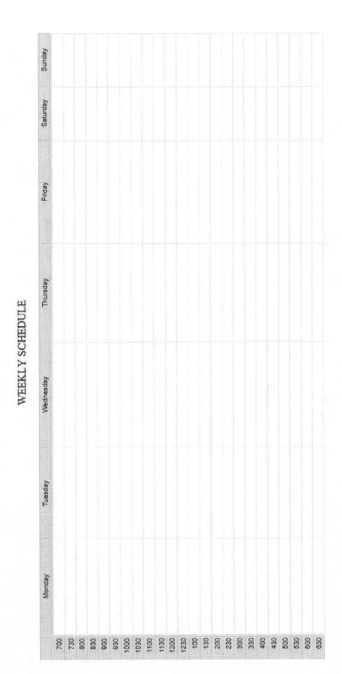

Delegation Roadmap

BOP Mission: to liberate small business owners from the chaos of working IN their business to the freedom of working ON their business.

First, either print out your own physical copy OR make a digital copy of this document within Google Drive.

I will walk you through each step first (see Steps 1 - 7), and then you will walk through the tool yourself to come up with a detailed list of your "Narrow Brilliance", and a list of things that you can delegate *right now*!

Step 1 - Write down *everything* you do currently in your role

Step 2 - Write down anything you *do not* currently do, but would like to

Step 3 - Answer two questions on every item from Step 1…
    1st Question - How much time does this take (in minutes) BOTH directly (time to actually do the task) and indirectly (time spent lamenting, correcting, or thinking about the task)

    2nd Question - Does this give you energy?

Up	This activity gives me energy
Nuetral	This activity neither gives or consumes energy
Down	This activity drains me of energy

    3rd Question - Do you *have* to do this or can someone else do it 80% as good as you after reasonable training?

1	*I* must do this

| 2 | I *feel like* I need to do this |
| 3 | I *could* delegate this to someone who could do it 80% as good as I can with reasonable training |

4th Question - How much is this task costing the business at my hourly rate?

Step 4 - Make a list of anything that is marked with an "up" arrow regardless of the response to the "2nd Question"

Step 5 - Make a list of anything that is ranked as a #2 or #3, and is either neutral or drains you of energy.

Step 6 - Take your list of Step 5 and begin delegating each item by answering these questions on each...
- Who has the capability to *own* this?
- How will I *train* the new owner of this?
- How will I *track*/account for progress?
- When will I *delegate* this?

Step 7 - Take your list from Step 4 and build your new role out of this list...this is your "Narrow Brilliance. Now build your new schedule around this list. Fight the voices in your head telling you, "It's not that easy!!!"

Who cares what *they* say! It is not *their* responsibility to live out what God has naturally put inside of you...it is yours alone.

Step 8 - IMPLEMENT AND DO IT!!

Organizational Chart

Common Systems	Additional Systems Needed	Final Systems List	Rank Current Health	Priority Moving Forward
Operations/Production	IT/Social Networking			
Customer Service				
Financial/Accounting				
Sales				
Marketing				
Talent/People (HR)				
Legal				
Communications				
Administration				

Master Process Roadmap

Example Process

"Systems are the big buckets, processes are how to do specific things"

1. **Trigger** (what action initiates this process?): *Thursdays at 2pm*

2. First step (once trigger happens what is the first step in this process?)
   a. Sub items within the first step
   b. Sub items within the first step
   c. SEE EXAMPLE SCRIPT BELOW

3. Next step (once trigger happens what is the first step in this process?)
   a. Sub items within the first step
   b. Sub items within the first step

4. Next step (once trigger happens what is the first step in this process?)
   a. Sub items within the first step
   b. Sub items within the first step

5. Next step (once trigger happens what is the first step in this process?)
   a. Sub items within the first step
   b. Sub items within the first step

EXAMPLE:

Trigger - Check Inventory Every Tuesday at 2p

1. Run a Kitchen Supply Inventory
   a. Cups
      i. If less than 40 cups

      ii.   Then Order 100 more
  b. Paper Towels
      i.   If less than 3 rolls
      ii.   Then Order 10 more
  c. Napkins
  d. Forks
  e. Knives
  f. Water Bottles

2. Order from _____ (using XYZ account username and password)
  a. Cups
  b. Paper Towels
  c. Napkins
  d. Forks
  e. Knives
  f. Water Bottles

Note - include share link of this process within the job role of whoever is responsible for implementation

Example Script to use if you needed to send a canned email

Greetings,

Jane Doe would like to order box lunches (half ham, half turkey) which include a sandwich, chips, bottled water, and a cookie to be delivered by (DATE) to (ADDRESS). Here are the dates & number of boxes...

5/5/16 - 6 people delivered by 12p

Please confirm this order has been received and send along online payment link.

Kind Regards,

(INSERT JANE'S SIGNATURE)

Team Meetings

Leader Name: _____

1. Mission and Values review (insert link to Vision, Mission, & Values document)

2. BIG (Begin In Gratitude) Win(s)
   a. Team Member Names Here
   b. _____
   c. _____
   d. _____

3. Accountability from last week's Action Items

4. This Week's Business Items
   a. Operations
      i. Project Task
      ii. Project Task
   b. Sales & Marketing
      i. Lead Follow Up
      ii. Conversion Metrics
   c. Administration
      i. Payables
      ii. Receivables
      iii. Cash On Hand

5. Action Items for next week (insert link to Action Items sheet)

6. Training
   a. Choose an internal process

Creating Your Process

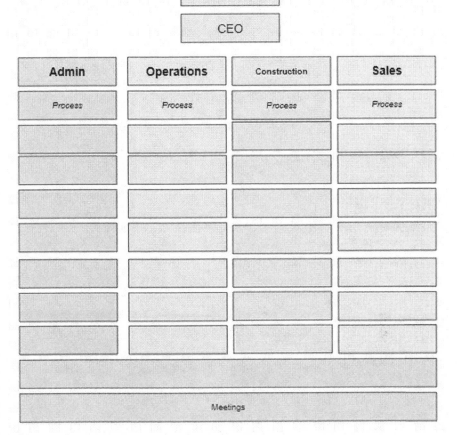

Level Two Dashboard

Accounts	January				
	All Numbers Below Are For Example Only				
	1/2/2019	1/9/2019	1/16/2019	1/23/2019	1/30/2019
All Income	$12,498.00	$200.00			
Profit* (Qtrly Draw in Green)	$22,318.00	$24,154.00			
Owner's Compensation	$8,435.00	$11,222.00			
Tax	$6,539.00	$7,978.00			
Operating Expense	$9,208.00	$8,776.00			
Sub-Total (subtract Taxes)	$45,920.00	$36,374.00			
Bookkeeping					
Quarterly Taxes Paid This Week					
Total Receivables	$53,049.04	$63,152.04			
Receivables Coming Due	$15,906.37	$23,706.37			
0-30	$15,620.66	$17,820.66			
30-60	$2,347.00	$4,000.00			
60-90	$5,000.00	$5,000.00			
over 90	$14,175.01	$12,625.01			
Payables Outstanding	$11,034.00	$8,356.00			
Debt Service Outstanding	$32,679.00	$30,658.00			
All In/Out Amount	$55,256.04	$91,170.04			
Customer (customize)					
Podcast Downloads	1346	1592			
Leads (non-referral)	2	3			
Conversions	1	0			
Referrals	3	3			
Follow Up Letters	4	4			

NOTES

1. https://www.simplemarketingnow.com/blog/flooring-the-consumer/bid/168520/What-Great-Brands-Do-With-Mission-Statements-8-Examples

2. https://www.google.com/webhp?sourceid=chrome-instant&ion=1&espv=2&ie=UTF-8#q=define%20 mission

3. https://www.biblegateway.com/passage/?search= Luke+14%3A25-34&version=NLT

34093759R00173

Made in the USA
Lexington, KY
18 March 2019